BATTLE OF THE ATLANTIC

An anthology of personal
memories from those
involved with the Battle of the Atlantic.

First published 1993 by Picton Press - Liverpool
1 & 3 Grove Road, Rock Ferry
Birkenhead, Wirral, Merseyside L42 3XS

Picton Press - Liverpool is the joint publishing imprint of The City of Liverpool - Libraries & Information Services. (part of the Leisure Directorate) & Countyvise Limited.

The City of Liverpool

ISBN 1 873245 04 1

Typeset & Printed by Birkenhead Press Limited
1 & 3 Grove Road, Rock Ferry
Birkenhead, Wirral, Merseyside L42 3XS

Cover design by: Chris Sarson (Liverpool Libraries & Information Services).

Dedication

This book is dedicated to those
who were lost at sea.
And whose stories remain untold.

I stuggled in the beginning. I said I was going to write the truth so help me God. And I thought I was. I found I couldn't. Nobody can write the absolute truth.

- Henry Miller

CONTENTS

Chapter 2

Chapter 3

Launch of the 'Ark Royal'.
The 'Ark Royal' was heavily used during the Battle of the Atlantic.

FOREWORD

This collection of personal accounts of the time of the Battle of the Atlantic illustrates a marvellous picture of the steadfastness and courage of the people of Merseyside. To read these moving accounts brings home, in a way only personal memories can, the truth of the phrase 'The People's War'. Individuals in a myriad of different occupations secured the nation's lifeline in the battle which was one of the very few that, if it had been lost, could have brought Britain to defeat. To those of us like myself who lived on Merseyside at the time, whether at home, or serving in the forces on land, at sea or in the air these stories not only bring back vivid memories, of both important and less significant things, but also cast light on activities which, unknown to us at the time, nevertheless contributed to final success. There are stories, too, of those who lost loved ones in the desperate struggle - a reminder that fifty years on, for very many, the grief remains.

This story portrays an important aspect of the nation's history, and will enable its' readers to understand how battles are won by ordinary men and women who attain the extrordinary when the existence of their nation is at stake.

Foreword by Sir Derek Bibby Bt, MC, DL
Chairman of Bibby Line Ltd of Liverpool 1969-1992

In May 1993 the City of Liverpool commemorates the 50th Anniversary of the ending of the Battle of the Atlantic. The Leisure Directorate (in conjunction with the Navy) has organised events to mark this occasion. The Libraries and Information Services' involvement in these events has been to collect these personal memories of the men and women involved. These stories have remained untold for fifty years.

Paul Catcheside
Chief Officer, Libraries & Information Services.

INTRODUCTION

It is with great pride we present this collection of personal memories from those involved or affected by the Battle of the Atlantic.

The Battle of the Atlantic was the longest running campaign of the Second World War. Its main purpose was to maintain the movement across the world of men, food and raw materials essential to Britain's survival. Liverpool played a major role in this - over 1000 convoys used the port. In 1941 Derby House in Exchange Flags, Liverpool, became the headquarters of the Western Approaches Command. This was the heart of the organisation of the Battle.

It has been said by many of the contributors to this book that the role of the Battle of the Atlantic in World War II and the role of Liverpool in this Battle has been underestimated. We hope the publication of this collection helps to remedy this.

One very important role of a library service is to collect and maintain a record of the history of the local community. Liverpool Libraries and Information Services (part of the Leisure Directorate in Liverpool) has aimed to do this by collecting these stories. We would like to thank everyone who contributed to this book and hope it will provide a source of interest and study for present day users and also become part of the setting down of the nations history for future generations.

Margo Storey
Project Co-ordinator

EDITING BOARD

Len Straughan, Elsie Pate, Chris Peach and Peter Lambe

Chapter 1
The Battle at Sea
.......In their own words

HMS TRACKER;THE WEATHER IS OUR WORST ENEMY

A lot has been written about the serious side of what went on in the Atlantic, especially by people who kept diaries, however, the lower deck ratings (like myself) were not allowed to keep diaries. You were made to believe it would be mortal sin to keep one. So my story is of a patrol that has no dates but happened in the Winter of 1943.

I was serving on HMS Tracker, an escort carrier attached to the Second Escort Group, with Captain Walker on his 'Starling' in command of the group. We had left the Clyde to join up with the rest of the group; HMS Starling - Wildgoose - Woodpecker - Kite -Magpie. Our patrol was to take us into the Atlantic down towards the Bay of Biscay and finally to Nova Scotia and Newfoundland.

The weather on this patrol was terrible, people who had been at sea for years were seasick. The ship had a roll and pitch they had not experienced before. On the ship at the time there was a reporter or war correspondent. An article of his appeared in the Daily Mirror. It was mostly about the weather and about the roll of the ship.

One night, when the weather was atrocious, there was a big explosion at the rear end of the ship; action stations was sounded. I made my way to the flight deck and was keeping a lookout on the starboard side of the ship. We thought the explosion could have been an acoustic torpedo going off before it hit us. I had experienced fear before during my five years in the Navy but I was frightened 'rigid' that night.

I was concentrating on a particular area of the ocean, every wave looked like a periscope, one particular wave (or White Horse) seemed to be coming faster towards the ship and was lasting longer. I imagined it was a torpedo. My heart must have been in my mouth because I couldn't utter a sound, which was just as well as that wave just broke away into the flow of water. Imagination can be a terrible thing. My fear was greater because it was night time. The six ships were now nearing Nova Scotia, and we were going to enter a place called Placentia. This was one of the bases occupied by the American Navy and on entering the harbour there was a band playing us in. Someone told them that the carrier, although the biggest ship, did not carry the Senior Captain. The quay was full of snow and ice, and to see these band members running along the convoy to find the 'Starling' with Captain Walker on board, was a sight for sore eyes. All credit to them, they were in position and ready to play when HMS Starling and the great Captain tied up.

Well this was one patrol where we did some chasing but hit nothing,we made up for that on the next patrol. *J. Allen*

DEATH IN THE AFTERNOON WATCH

October was here again, October 1942 - and with it came the winter storms. Not that a Summer storm in the North Atlantic is so very different from a Winter storm. A Summer storm may feel a bit warmer, but it can scatter a convoy just as quickly as a Winter storm.

The year 1942 was a bad year for Allied merchant shipping and losses were heavy. As well as that, we had the 'black gap' where air cover could not reach.

The Western Approaches B6 group had secured alongside at Argentia, Newfoundland after escorting ON132 over the Atlantic and were thankful for a few days rest. The group consisted of the destroyer HMS 'Viscount' S.O. (Cdr John Waterhouse, RN) and the Norwegian corvettes KNM 'Potentilla' (Lt. Cdr. Chr. Monsen, RNN) 'Eglantine' (Lt Cdr H Valtersvik, RNN), 'Montbretia' (Lt. Cdr H. Soiland, RNN) and 'Acanthus (Lt. Bruen, RNN).

When at Argentia, the group was strengthened by the addition of the destroyer HMS 'Fame' (Cdr. S. Heathcote, RN) who became Senior Officer. The Norwegian 'Rose' had been detached to support a south-going convoy on its way to Gibraltar after which 'Rose' was to return to Liverpool.

Slow Convoy

On the morning of October 9 the group sailed from Argentia to take over escorting the east going convoy SC104 from the Local Western Escort Force. This convoy consisted of 48 merchant ships and the rescue ship 'Stretcher', and had an advance speed of seven knots. This was considered a slow convoy.

Air cover was present until the evening of October 12 but a signal from Admiralty warned that at least two U-boats appeared to have sighted the convoy. This news was bad news.

The escorts had taken up the following escort positions: 'Fame', 'Montbretia' and 'Eglantine' to starboard and 'Potentilla' and 'Acanthus' to port. HMS 'Viscount' was covering the front of the convoy. The weather was bad. A northwest storm was blowing and, at intervals, snow showers. High seas which broke on board the corvettes made watch keeping a wet job and, as well as this, reduced visibility and speed when this was required. In between the snow showers, visibility was good. During the day the S.O.'s HF/DF began to register several contacts and it was assumed that more U-boats were in contact or on their way to SC104.

The first sinking was on the night of October 13 when the Norwegian ship 'Fagersten' was sunk with all hands at 04.25 and at 05.08 another Norwegian ship, the 'Senta' was also sunk. So far, no direct contact had been made between the escorts and the enemy, but it was clear to all that we had a wolf pack snarling around the convoy.

When daylight came, the escorts began to obtain contacts and several attacks and searches were carried out and this meant that, as darkness fell, only 'Fame', 'Monbretia' and 'Acanthus' were now protecting the convoy. These three ships had both visual and Asdic contacts and attacked with gunfire and depth charges.

Due to weather conditions and high seas it was almost impossible to see from the bridge of a corvette and when a U-boat was sighted, these conditions so reduced speed that the U-boat could dive and disappear before contact could be obtained with Asdic.

On the night of October 13/14 the wolf pack attacks began at 22.15 and kept going until 02.30. During this period, the whale factory ship MS 'Southern Empress' was torpedoed but, in spite of this and a list, she kept going at six knots. The convoy course was now 065 degrees.

The three escorts still remaining with the convoy were now positioned: 'Montbretia' to starboard, 'Acanthus' to port and 'Fame' astern. 'Viscount', 'Eglantine' and 'Potentilla' were about 25 miles astern but rejoining at full speed.

It was with this convoy, although I am not certain on which night, the following incident happened.

Smiles were few

Thinking about it now I can smile, but at the time smiles were few and far between. There was a snow storm blowing, taking the tops off the waves and sending them against the dodgers like machine gun bullets.

I was standing on the starboard end of the bridge, endeavouring to keep a watch when, suddenly, the Asdic Petty Officer came running our of the Asdic hut to the starboard side beside me and began peering over the side and astern.

I watched him in amazement. Suddenly he turned to me and shouted: 'Did you see it, Sir?' Still peering aft he shouted: 'An MTB, Sir - passed down the starboard side at full speed.'

This information was amazing due to position and weather conditions and shows how heavy the weather in a corvette can reduce normal understanding. Tapping the PO on the shoulder I shouted: 'An MTB, in the middle of the Atlantic and in a snow storm?' He slowly righted himself up and stood looking at me: 'An MTB? Bloody Hell, it must have been a torpedo!'

It was perhaps as well that the bridge was several inches deep in water otherwise the Petty Officer's feet might have burnt holes with the speed he made back to his station.

The northern lights were very active and when these were rolling in the sky, visibility became four miles. At 22.15 the British ship 'Susana' was sunk.

HMS 'Viscount' was now about two miles astern when she sighted a U-boat, on the surface right ahead. She opened fire and prepared to ram, but the U-boat managed to steer clear at the last moment so 'Viscount' fired 14 depth charges as she passed over the spot but, after this, could not establish contact.

During the night, the 'Nellie' and the 'Nikoline Matkonik' were sunk. During this attack the 'Monbretia' obtained a visual contact but again high seas made it impossible to keep contact when the boat dived.

'Potentilla', who had earlier picked up 10 men adrift in a lifeboat, was, at first light, again ordered astern to search for survivors. During the night the 'Southern Empress' had been torpedoed again and had sunk within five minutes.

After searching, 'Potentilla' sent a signal to the S.O., 'that the sea astern of the convoy is littered with lifeboats and rafts containing survivors' and requesting the rescue ship as high seas made if difficult to rescue these men. The S.O. sent a signal ordering the 'Potentilla' to stay and give protection to the 'Stretcher' when she arrived. During the day 'Potentilla' returned to the convoy with 82 men on board, most of them taken up from the crew of the 'Southern Empress'. And so the fight went on, searching attacking and guarding.

The last ship sunk was the 'Empire Mersey' which was hit by two torpedoes.

The afternoon of October 15 was one of those days. Old man Atlantic was resting in his corner but we knew that at any minute he would come out again with both fists up ready for another slugging match. But now, he was resting and the sun was shining.

I remember the bridge was rather crowded with those who had come up to enjoy the sunny weather. Even some of the engine personnel had come up on deck to have a look. These boys always seemed to come from another world. There they stood, close to the engine room entrance and bunched together. Now and then they would look up at the bridge, then look at the depth charge throwers, now study the pom pom and the horizon, always as if all this was a dangerous place to be. One second they were there and the next, they were gone, back to the shining metal, the spotless white enamel and the heat of the engine room. Here they felt safe which always seems strange with U-boats around. We all stood and enjoyed the sight of the convoy behaving as it should.

"SO in contact"

'Senior Officer in contact' - the voice of the signalman brought us up all standing and binoculars where turned onto the destroyer.

She was moving away from the convoy with her black signal flag flying.

'Attacking'. Again the signalman's voice spelt out the news.

The bowwave of the destroyer began to rise and her stern boiled and began to sink as she gained speed.

'Depth charges away'. Silently we waited for the bangs and soon we saw the columns of water rise and our hull shuddered from the explosions.

Now we waited to see the result. We had seen this all before, many, many times - mostly at night - first the contact, the slow closing towards the contact with the ping getting shorter and shorter, then the 'full speed' and then the 'fire'.

After this circle and the search for a renewed contact and then the searching until the signal came; 'Resume station'.

So now we waited.

'Krriist' - a gasp went up. Something was breaking the surface.

Something black, dirty, ugly and dangerous. A U-boat.

'Fame' was now closing the enemy to ram and we saw her stem press the U-boat down before she broke clear. The boat soon appeared again and the destroyer opened fire.

We were so astonished that the order 'open fire' came as a shock.

Soon the bridge Oerlikons were chattering and we could see the sparks of hits coming from the conning tower.

The crew began abandoning the sinking boat, jumping into the water and swimming towards 'Acanthus'. Some were swimming well but others were making a bad job of it and we could see their heads getting lower and lower in the water. One boy kept shouting and appeared to been in a bad way but he was still making for us.

The scramble net was put out and the Germans who reached it began coming on board. They were wet and cold and all their fight had disappeared. One of the first to come on board was a Czech who had been conscripted into the German Navy. He was in good form and was delighted to be on deck and did all he could to help his shipmates, but we had a problem. The Germans were cold and shivering and could do little to help get their wet leather uniforms off before being sent down to the lock up. The leather belts holding up their leather trousers were impossible to open, but one of the Norwegian crew found a solution. Pulling out his sheath knife he cut the belt and them moved on to the next man. The first German knew what was happening but the next only saw a large Norwegian coming at him with a sheath knife as if he was about to do him an injury and his screams shook us up. The lad who was making bad weather of it, at last reached the scrambling net.. He managed to grab it but the roll tore him clear and he went under. The next time he had a chance he again managed to grab hold but again a roll tore him loose from the net.

Suddenly the water around him became white with vomit and he began to sink.

There was a boat hook hand and we managed to hook him but his uniform tore and with his hands up his lifebelt came off. There was nothing more we could do except stand and watch. To begin with we could see the green uniform but this gradually began to disappear. After a few seconds only the white face was visible in the clear green water, before this too disappeared.

The ship began to move and we were off again to investigate a new possible contact and then rejoin the convoy.

As we passed, the dead, still floating in the water on their lifebelts, turned towards us and nodded before beginning their lonely *dance macabre.*

LL. Cmdr C.Bain,RNR

THE STORY OF TWO ANTI-SUBMARINE TRAWLERS

In 1936, the 650 ton trawlers 'Northern Gem' and 'Northern Spray', two of a group of fifteen similar trawlers being built at Bremerhaven, Germany. joined Grimsby's distant waters' fishing fleet and began their peacetime occupation of hunting prime fish in the Arctic Ocean, Barents, and White Seas.

By September 1939 this hazardous, although peaceful activity came to a sudden end when the trawlers were requisitioned by the Admiralty, equipped with submarine detection equipment, armed with a full compliment of depth charges, a four inch gun and sundry anti-aircraft weaponry, and sent to war as two of His Majesty's minor war vessels.

After exemplary service on Northern patrol in the winter of 1939-40, and the ill fated Norwegian campaign of April-June 1940, together with anti-invasion night patrols in the English Channel in the summer of 1940, the trawlers then began convoy escort duties, which were to take up most of their sea time for the remainder of the war.

Commanded by officers of the R.N.R. and R.N.V.R., and with crews ofthe Royal Naval Patrol Service - men from all walks of life, included quite a few from Liverpool and district - the trawlers became increasingly efficient in this responsible work.

Beginning with convoys to and from the U.K. and Iceland, the trawlers then became part of the close escorts of convoys to North Russia in 1942, accompanying Convoys PQ16, PQ17, JW51B and Operation" FB", all of which were subjected to fierce attacks by enemy aircraft and U-boats, suffering grievous losses of ships and men.

H.M.S. Northern Gem in 1942. A 650-ton trawler formerly a fishing boat was requisitioned in the Battle of the Atlantic.

As 1943 dawned, with increasing quantities of both armaments and men being shipped across the Atlantic in preparation for 'D Day', the Battle of the Atlantic moved towards its climax. At this time the two trawlers were attached to the experienced and efficient Escort Group B7 under the leadership of Sir Peter Gretton in the destroyer 'Duncan', fulfilling a dual role as part screen round the convoys, and also acting as rescue ships.

In May 1943, whilst escorting a 42-ship outward-bound convoy, ONS5,the group became engaged in an epic battle which ultimately was recognised as a triumph. In a conflict which raged over nine days and nights, with no less than an estimated forty U-boats in contact with the convoy, and during which twelve merchant ships were torpedoed and sunk, B7 Escort Group, assisted by Support Group reinforcement and long range aircraft, sank six of the attacking Uboats with two more U-boats lost in collision. Losses of forty three U-boats during that decisive month of May 1943, forced Admiral Doenitz to withdraw his U-boats from the North Atlantic. Northern Spray was kept very busy rescuing survivors form the torpedoed merchantmen and finally steamed into St John's, Newfoundland with one hundred and forty three British, American, Norwegian, Filipino and Lascar seamen on board.

After landing the survivors, cleaning ships, re-arming and making the ships ready for sea again, a signal was received from His Majesty King George VI which must surely rank with Nelsonian signals of an earlier age, "To all officers and men of Escort Group B7-Well done. Splice the main brace." George R.I.

E.H. Bardsley, Telegraphist
RNV (W) R H. M. S. Northern Spray

THE WOLF OF THE ATLANTIC

On 14 March 1941, HMS 'Walker', in company with our sister ship HMS' Vanoc' rounded up the ships which were to be our Convoy. There were twenty two ships altogether, convoy number HX112, as we set sail from Halifax, Nova Scotia for Britain.

For the first couple of days we had one or two U-boat alarms and dropped single depth charges just to let the submarines know that we were aware of their proximity. Admiralty Intelligence informed us that Admiral Doenitz, on the orders of Hitler, was assembling a ' Wolf Pack' of U-boats as Hitler wanted this convoy completely destroyed to show German supremacy in the Atlantic.

At dusk on Saturday 15 March, a freighter on our side of the convoy was torpedoed. We did not detect any submarine but continued the sweep as we did not want to wander too far from the convoy and leave it unprotected. You must realise that due to the shortage of men and ships at this time, only two First World War destroyers could be spared for this convoy. On Sunday we lost another ship; this time it was a tanker from the centre of the convoy. HMS 'Vanoc' had a submarine contact and she attacked with depth charges but after losing contact she rejoined the convoy.

The forenoon of Monday 17 March, St Patrick's Day, started off badly. We were attacked from both sides and lost three ships. From the submarine echo's that our Asdic operators were picking up,. we came to the conclusion that we were now under attack from the expected "Wolf Pack". The attack continued throughout the afternoon and we lost two more freighters and another tanker. My God, to see a tanker torpedoed is to see "Hell on Earth"; to watch shipmates jump from one blazing hell into another (a blazing sea) and be helpless to aid them, is terrible.

Just before midnight, our sister ship 'Vanoc' reported that she had a Radar contact which could only be a submarine in the surface. This was the first time that Radar had been used as it was still in its infancy. Our Captain, being the senior officer, ordered the 'Vanoc' to attack the contact. As she was too close to drop depth charges, 'Vanoc' rammed the U-boat, which was the U100 captained by one of the top U-boat aces, Schepke. He, being in the conning tower as they collided, was cut in two. Suddenly our Asdic operator, Backhouse, called out 'Bridge, submarine!' and gave the bearing. Our Captain Donald McIntyre, checked the bearing and told the operator, 'You are picking up the 'Vanoc'. Backhouse replied, 'No sir, it is definitely a submarine.' The Captain then ordered the yeomen of signals to tell the 'Vanoc' to ' get the hell out of it, you are sitting over a submarine!'

The 'Vanoc' disentangled herself from the submarine U100 and made off as best she could. We immediately went into the attack and dropped a pattern of six depth charges, did a 180 degree turn straight over where we considered the submarine to be and dropped another pattern of depth charges. As we swung round again, the submarine suddenly broke the surface and as her gun's crew ran towards their gun, I ordered our gun's crew to open fire. The U-boat started sinking stern first. Suddenly the Captain called across in plain English 'Please save my crew.' Captain McIntyre said, 'Let the bastards sink!' Don't forget we were in the heat of battle and had lost good men and ships, and some of them to a horrible death. Then he ordered us to throw over the scrambling nets and we drifted over towards the submarine, ourselves now a sitting duck for any other U-boats in the vicinity. We were off Iceland and death was quick in those waters. The sinking submarine was U-99 and her captain was Otto Kretschmer, the top U-boat ace, known as 'The Wolf of the Atlantic.'

We placed the prisoners in the galley flat under escort as we had nowhere else to put them and we were still fighting off submarines. As dawn broke, we brought the convoy back into line, then we assembled the prisoners on the upper deck and paraded them up and down the lines of merchant ships to the cheers of the brave merchant seamen who had survived the battle. When the Germans saw the number of ships still afloat, they could not believe their eyes! The convoy continued to Liverpool and, on reaching the Bar, we left the convoy and made for the Pier Head where we tied up alongside to more cheering.

The prisoners that we brought ashore were the first German submarine prisoners to be taken and brought into Britain. We landed them at the Pier Head and turned them over to the Army. They started to march them towards Lime Street Station where a special train was waiting to take them to London. The crowds of women who were watching started screaming and tried to attack them, so the Army called for a lorry and took them to Walton prison where they spent the night and were shipped off in the morning to London. One must understand this was Liverpool and quite a number of these men who had been lost so far, both Merchant and Royal Navy, came from Liverpool. Some of those men lost were sons and husbands of the women in the crowd.

I should mention that during this battle, the Admiralty kept inquiring what the losses were on both sides, and the names of the submarine Captains, if known. Winston Churchill announced the details that morning in Parliament but Hitler did not tell the German people for almost three months that his three top aces were dead or had been taken prisoner.

Since the end of the war and the release of prisoners, the survivors of both sides of the battle have visited our respective countries and have become friends. On the British side, we have only nine known survivors still alive. In September last year, I received a card from Otto Kretschmer, now Admiral of the German Navy, and the surviving crew members of his submarine U-99, who gave a party to celebrate his 80th birthday - the card was signed by all those present.

I would like to mention that in later years, when talking to Jupp Kassals, the radio operator of U-99, he said that when we handed them over to the Army as prisoners, he had been more afraid of the women who threatened to attack them than he had been when we had been attacking their submarine with depth charges or swimming for his life in the icy sea!

This all happened a long time ago but is still fresh in my memory. I might add that later in the war in 1944, I was sunk in the Atlantic while on a sister ship HMS 'Warwick', by submarine U-413. Fortunately, I was saved but 67 of my shipmates were lost. They will be in my thoughts at the commemorative service in Liverpool Cathedral.

William Douglas Aldridge Begg M.I.D.
Ex Chief Petty Officer, G.I. Royal Navy

EXPERIENCES IN A LIFEBOAT

Three mates and myself were on a ship called the 'Oronsey' heading home to England from South Africa. One night while asleep, we were torpedoed, two in succession hitting the ship. There were about two thousand people on board all going home. They were screaming and running in all directions. We could smell the cordite fumes. Everybody was rushing for the lifeboats. The third torpedo struck. People were in life boats but there were no crew members in them to show them what to do. My friend and I jumped into the water and finally go in a lifeboat. Our other two friends were lost that night.

After a couple of days the sun was burning hot and men in the boat were badly burnt and blistered. We had to row the boat, and after awhile our backs were aching, and the water was rationed. After awhile we decided to row at night as it was so hot through the day. There were a few airmen in our boat, and one man was a real morale booster. He would recite poems, and keep the men's spirits up. By this time the water was very low, and tongues were swollen, and all of us badly sunburnt. He died after a few days, saying the Lord's Prayer. He had recited before he died 'If' by Rudyard Kipling. There were sharks in the water and one day one attacked the boat. It was about 20 ft long, a hammer head shark. It rocked the boat then went back under the water. To pass the time away I used to think of all the places I had been to while a merchant seaman, every country and town, a hundred places and more. The mental anguish we went through; we thought we would be better off dead. It was the 15th day and we had used up all our water. Men were moaning and mumbling. I myself was rambling, and thought I had seen and spoken to my brother who had been killed in the Blitz on Liverpool, but I had been hallucinating.

After three weeks someone said they heard a plane and it was in the distance. We sent a flare up and the plane came nearer. It was a deafening sound after the silence of the past weeks. This plane was a Sunderland Flying Boat looking for survivors of ships, and was on its way back when it had seen our flare. It was a few days before we were picked up by the destroyer 'Brilliante'. The Commander was telling us through the tannoy to stand by and sailors helped all of us on board where we lay on the decks. We had to hurry away as we were sitting ducks for the enemy. It was quite an operation. We were all ill, but feeling wonderful, and so grateful to everybody, we all wept.

EDWIN BENN

The above story is taken from tapes my brother left me, there's a lot more to it but I have picked out the story line. I've written it like he is saying it. He was torpedoed a few times on different ships and was many years in the Merchant Navy.

MRS FREDA CHADWICK

JOINING THE QUEEN MARY

I sailed on the 'Alaunia' out of Huskisson Dock in March 1940 to join our ship the 'Queen Mary' which had lain in 92 pier in New York (The Cunard Berth). We stayed in a hotel in New York called the Cornish Arms.

The Queen Mary was under observation from the German Embassy at all times, 24 hours around the clock. The morning we arrived at New York; March 18th 1940 was a cold morning. The New York Times had a big headline on its front page 'British Tars arrive to take over 'Queen Mary'". There were thousands of people down at the pier who were kept on the move by squads of mounted police. The painters came on board her and painted her Battle Grey. Then, a couple of nights later the 'Queen Elizabeth' slipped into the next berth. I was ashore and watched her arrive.

When I went on board the 'Queen Mary' I was put on watches right away. On her deck and in the engine room we set about our duties. She sailed on my watch, during the early hours on the 12 - 4 watch. She slipped out of New York Harbour. The biggest ship in the world at that time.

John Bennett

LUCKY TO BE ALIVE

The year was 1942, I was at the Pier head when I heard they were looking for seamen to sail on the R.M.S. 'Laconia'. I had seen her before as an armed cruiser for the Navy. The armament was substantial and I thought this would be a safe ship to sail on. I went to the Cunard Building and signed on as a seaman.

We embarked troops for the Middle East going in convoy around the Cape up the east coast of Africa to the Suez. The return trip saw us sailing alone; with Italian P.O.W.'s, troops going on leave and some women and children passengers. We left Cape Town retracing our course down the East coast of Africa around the cape and up the West Coast headed for Freetown. September 12th started as a routine day;we had doubled the lookouts for submarines. One man on the foredeck and one in the crow's nest on watch. I had the 8-12 watch on the foredeck; it was about seven fifty five pm when I went on deck to relieve my shipmate who's name was Bob, I don't remember his last name. He said 'There's nothing around Al,' and down below he went. That was the last time I saw Bob. At sunset there was as light sea with small white caps. I took a look around the horizon, saw nothing and turned towards the bridge. It was now eight o five; that was when the first torpedo hit us below the bridge on the starboard side. I stood there in disbelief at what had just happened, and the next one hit. I was standing there wondering what I should do when the ship's whistle blasted out six short blasts and one long blast, the signal for abandon ship. I made my way up to the boat deck. My boat was #12 which was alongside the radio room, there I joined up with Bob Gillion, a seaman from Liverpool. Together we put her in the water, he lowered the aft end and I lowered the bow. It was then the radio operator came and asked if we could do anything with the main aerial that was now down. Gillion said to me 'Let's see if they have gotten the wireless boats away,' so we went aft (where they were stationed). The port boat was still in it's chocks and with the ship's list we could not move it. Moving across the deck the starboard boat was still there, so we put her in the water. We had to get the motor started so we shouted for the engineer, I don't know who came down but he soon had the motor running. We pulled away from the ship which was now down at the bow and listing heavily to starboard. When we were clear of her we shut the motor down. We then put up the mast, pulled up the radio aerial and sent out a signal. We did not know if the signal would reach as the set had a maximum range of about 500 miles. Shortly after the signal went out we heard a high pitched motor. Looking in the direction of the sound we saw the sub coming towards us, we then pulled down the aerial knowing the U-boat wouldn't want our position known. He passed us not more than fifty feet away.

The next morning we picked up one of our seamen, Mike Coogan, he was from the south end of Liverpool; he was sitting on a small raft. Later we drifted up to a waterlogged boat, in it was Second Officer Mr Rose, Hurst the purser and six others who we took aboard. We could not take the P.O.W.'S that were there as we now had very little freeboard. With the boat's repair kit we tacked up canvas around the side of the boat that kept the spray out. The boat, which I think was supposed to hold 28 people was now holding 45 or more, one of which was a young girl about 12 years of age. We asked Mr Rose for a course, he gave us North East. We put up the sail and were on our way.

The morning of the sixteenth we sighted an object on the horizon; we were hoping it was one of our destroyers, but as she came closer we saw it was a sub flying the Italian flag. We nearly died, she was the Italian submarine 'Cappelline'. Coming alongside we were asked where the other boats were, and if we had any Italians on board. We told them they were on the other boats, Mr Rose gave them the position where the ship went down. They gave us six bottles of wine, six bottles of water; they wished us good luck and went on their way.

The next morning we were the first picked up by the Vichy French cruiser 'Glorie'. The cruiser continued to search over the vast area for a day to a day and a half to pick up the rest of the boats. She sailed to Casablanca where we were interned until the North African invasion, finishing at the French Foreign Legion camp at the Atlas mountains. We were the lucky ones, some of our shipmates who were saved by U-boat 156 were later killed when a U.S. Liberator bomber attacked the U-boat while she was towing survivors in the lifeboat.

Albert Beyer

CONSTANT RAIN AND HEAVY SEAS

From 1941 to 1945 I was a young apprentice/cadet aboard tramp ships belonging to a firm of London shipowners, Messrs Watts, Watts & Co. These ships were coal burners and, if we were lucky, could steam at about eight knots, which was fairly average for tramp ships in those days. They were always dirty and often rusty as well. Life aboard was never comfortable; food was scarce and, as I recall, we lads were always hungry. The work was hard and very basic. For every seaman there was never any let-up in tension once we were sea.

Between 1941 and the end of 1943 I sailed in about ten convoys across the North Atlantic, most of which either started or finished at Liverpool.

I was one of those lucky individuals who never had a ship sunk under them nor ever had to jump for his life into an open lifeboat. But I was often an unwilling witness to the sinking of many fine ships from those convoys.

Funnily enough, my most vivid memories of convoy work in the North Atlantic are not those of U-boat attacks, or alarms, or sinkings but of the awful weather conditions under which we sailed throughout almost every voyage I made. My memories are of high swells and of ships rolling and pitching every which way as they fought to stay in position in the convoy. The hurricane force winds and almost constant rain together with the heavy seas that came crashing aboard made the main decks an almost constant river. No matter how well we, as watch keepers, wrapped up, against the conditions, the rain could always find a way in, seeping into our seaboots; dribbling around the collars of our so'wester oilskins and dripping down our necks. I think we hated the weather almost as much as we hated the submarines.

Perhaps my most enduring recollection of the Battle of the Atlantic is centred around Christmas Day and Boxing Day 1943 when, sailing as part of a convoy bound for Russia, we were nearly intercepted by the German battleship 'Scharnhorst' which had sortied from it's lair intending to sink every last one of us. Fortunately for us we were well protected by the Navy and the story of the Battle of the Barents Sea is now history. For 48 hours we spent many an anxious moment unaware of our near escape, but very aware as we stood to action stations throughout that arctic day, that 'something was up'. We saw the occasional flashes of the big guns and heard the distant rumble as the convoy carried out a series of emergency turns, first one way, then another, like a hare trying to escape the hounds.

In the event, Germany lost the 'Scharnhorst' and we lost our Christmas dinner. We had all been far too nervous and excited, and with the weather again at its atrocious worst, we only celebrated that Holy Day with cold sandwiches and hot tea. Never mind, we made up for it with a bang-up feast to combine Christmas and New Year after we had arrived, safe and sound in Murmansk.

I have recollections of the south Atlantic too; of sunny days, blue skies, flying fish, clam seas and indescribably beautiful moonlit nights. But that was when I also remember ships being sunk; for it was a happy hunting ground for submarines throughout the whole war and almost every convoy I sailed in had at least one casualty.

After 1943 I spent the rest of the war aboard a ship that regularly carried army stores. We ferried tanks, lorries and ammunition up and down the Mediterranean, visiting landing beaches and invasions with supplies for our advancing armies. From the beaches of Southern France we took nearly 1000 German and Italian prisoners of war to their camps in Egypt; they were an unhappy lot of men.

I managed to arrive home in April 1945 and was able to join in a great all-night dancing and singing jamboree on St George's Plateau, Liverpool on the night of VE Day. I remember being in a huge conga line of servicemen and women, and civilians. Almost all allied nationalities seemed to be represented as we danced through Gerrard Gardens to celebrate the end of the war and the war at sea.

Michael Blackmon

CONVOY DUTIES IN THE ATLANTIC

In 1940, I was a first class stoker serving on board a destroyer HMS'Keppel', a flotilla leader engaged on convoy duties in the Atlantic and Western Approaches.. We were also doing Malta convoys and North Russian convoys. During these convoys in the Atlantic the sea was that rough we could only see the convoy when we were on top of the waves, and in the boiler rooms we had to wear our oilskins to keep dry as the sea kept coming in through the fan shafts. On 11th May we rescued survivors of the SS 'Somerset' which had been bombed and sunk by aircraft; again we rescued survivors from the Norwegian ship MV 'Vigrid' which had been torpedoed and sunk by a U-boat on June 24th. In much calmer weather we broke down for two hours. We had trouble with one of the main bearings, and had to replace it with a new one. We made so much noise that everyone was on pins in case we too were torpedoed. All went well and we were on our way to pick up the convoy. We were near it when we saw a U-boat trailing behind. We almost caught up with it, when it saw us and dived. We dropped depth charges till we thought we had got it, we saw patches of oil but nothing else.

In June 1942 we were sent on convoy PQ17 to Russia and we had to supply the guns with 56 lb shells. My station was on Y Gunshaft. It was then I saw a torpedo coming towards us, I shouted to the gun crew and they reported it to the bridge. Our Captain, Commander Jack Broome, turned hard to port and the torpedo missed us by inches. When HMS 'Eagle' was torpedoed we helped to pick up survivors. It was a terrible convoy, but I was mostly in the boiler room, sweating. When HMS 'Kenya' was hit we had to take the survivors and escort HMS 'Kenya' back to GB.

Battle Honours

Atlantic	1940 1943
Malta	1942
Arctic	1942-45
English Channel	1944
Normandy	1944

U-boats sunk by HMS 'Keppel'

U-229	U-343
U-763	U-394
U-360	U-713

Harry Brown

DEFENSIVELY EQUIPPED MERCHANT SHIPS (D.E.M.S.)

I was an able seaman and gunner on a D.E.M.S. and served on the RMS 'Queen Elizabeth' when she sailed without a convoy to Halifax, Nova Scotia, and New York, U.S.A. We sailed westwards with very few passengers on board; they were mainly servicemen and women who were returning to Canada or the U.S.A. on leave. We filled up with American and Canadian military personnel, about 17,000 of them, for the return voyage to Gourock, Scotland. After leaving the 'Lizzie' I joined the SS 'Empire Flamingo' and went to North Africa to support the Eighth Army. I received the Atlantic Star, the Africa Star and the Eighth Army Clasp.

Able Seaman and Gunner Frank Bunn aged 19 who received the Atlantic Star, the Africa Star and the Eigth Army clasp.

One incident in particular from these years remains vividly in my mind. All the gunners kept watch, four hours on and eight hours off. We would stand in the gun pits keeping a look-out with our guns at the ready. We did not sail due West but zig-zagged to avoid submarines. One day, a Canadian serviceman who was going home on leave after two years in

Europe, fell over the side. The captain gave orders that the ship could not stop; if we stopped, we could be a target for any U-boats in the area. I watched as the service man became a small dot in the vastness of the ocean. Many other servicemen will understand the feelings of helplessness as I witnessed this incident. As the war progressed, it was a feeling that I experienced again and again.

Frank D. Bunn

MY FIRST TRIP

It was a cold February day in 1940 and snow was thick on the ground as I made my way down to the Langton Dock to join the SS 'Barnhill', a tramp steamer of 5000 tons. She was at least 40 years old and as dirty and rusty as an old bucket, but I was excited as I was about to embark on my first trip as a seventeen year old cabin boy. The war was only five months old and far from my mind, but I was in for a rude awakening!

We sailed from the dock in ballast on a bitterly cold day to join a convoy whose destination was unknown as yet. We were unable to do more than 8 knots and frequently dropped to as low as 6 because, with the ship being empty, the propeller often rose out of the water, and reduced the speed of the ship. Time and time again we fell behind the convoy until we were told to proceed on our own. Six hours later the engines broke down completely and we were left drifting helplessly until they were repaired. We managed to join another convoy but broke down again and finished the journey alone. Each time we broke down all the crew were scared because we were sitting ducks for U-boats or enemy planes, but 'Lady Luck' finally smiled on us - the freezing weather changed to warm sunny days when the ocean was like a mill-pond and we made better speed. U-boats were not operating as far as we had reached this early in the war - only armed raiders like the 'Graf Spee' and fortunately we did not encounter any of them.

Finally we were told that our destination was the West Indies and a few days later we sailed into the harbour of Barbados and began loading 6000 tons of brown sugar for the U.K. On the journey back, it was the same story, either breaking down or steaming too slowly to keep up with the rest of the convoy and we had to go it alone. Nearing home, a convoy ahead of us was attacked and several ships were sunk. We passed miles of wreckage but could not stop for fear of being sunk ourselves. We made slow progress until we were a day or so from home when we joined up with a small convoy of about six ships which were all as slow as we were. Suddenly, two German planes came out of the sky and attacked the convoy; two ships were hit and sunk but we escaped. On the next day we arrived at Millwall Docks, unloaded our cargo, and were paid off. Now, fifty-three years later, when I put sugar in my tea I think of the SS 'Barnhill' and her cargo, and how glad I was to get home in one piece.

J Carroll

THE BIGGEST DANGER - THE ATLANTIC STORMS

Even now, 50 years on, I still have quite vivid memories of the Battle of the Atlantic. At that time I was serving as a Leading Coder on board HMS 'Fame'. She was Senior Officer of Escort Group B6 from 1942 until 1944 and during that time escorted 26 Atlantic convoys.

I suppose the most vivid memory must be of the weather, especially those winter storms. Hurricane force winds scattered the convoys in all directions, sinking ships or causing them to heave-to and doing tremendous damage to the escort vessels. The seas were enormous... davits were uprooted; seaboats were smashed to matchwood; guard rails were flattened and gun shields bent beyond recognition. Ice was another problem. It wou!d cover the superstructure, freeze the guns and depth charges and the weight of it would often threaten to capsize the ship.

The U-boat danger ran second to Mother Nature at her worst, but 'Fame' with her other escort vessels, had their share of luck in sinking or damaging U-boats. In our Escort Group, we had five corvettes manned entirely by Norwegian crews and how they hated the Nazis! They would follow a contact for hours and hours and claimed several U-boats sunk or badly damaged. One outstanding memory is of the 'Fame' ramming and sinking a U-boat in full view of the convoy. In fact, as the merchantmen sailed past our position, the D.E.M.S. gunners opened fire at the sinking U-boat. I think we were more in danger of this gunfire than the U-boat, and the Captain quickly ordered them to 'cease fire'!

Another memory of this trip, was of the concern the whole ships' company had for its 'rabbits'. 'Rabbit' was the word used to describe the presents we were taking home to our families. Silk stockings, underwear, candies, toys and 'Lux' toilet soap were all on their way home for Christmas 1942, and none had a more eventful crossing, as both 'Fame' and 'Viscount', (another destroyer escort), both rammed and sunk U-boats which caused severe flooding below decks, but Liverpool was safely reached and the 'rabbits' passed through customs!

But my greatest memory is of reaching home and being greeted by my wife with our new born daughter... born on the day we had been in action with the U-boat. She is looking over my shoulder as I write this.

Liwut Commander (Sp) A. G. Coles VRD., RNR (Rtd)

U-BOAT HUNTERS

I was serving on HMS 'Lossie', which was Canadian built, when we began an Atlantic convoy from Bermuda. Then we joined the U-boat Walkers Group which was based at Londonderry. We were fitted with the Hedgehog Bomb Throwers searching for U-boats on the 30 degree Atlantic, sweeping in front of convoys going East and West. There were 16 frigates and stoops steaming, lines abreast, at five miles apart. An Auxiliary aircraft carrier accompanied us in order to refuel us at sea, this then meant that we were able to stay at sea for about three weeks. We could usually 'bag' seven or eight U-boats at a sweep and this figure does not include the many 'probables'. When we arrived back in Londonderry, all the depth charges and bombs were spent. The charge spaces were filled with U-boat men - some were not so lucky. At that time, the winter 1942/3, the Germans started using Acoustic torpedoes which were able to pick up the sound of propellers and which usually blew ships sterns off.

Mr A S Coupeland
(ex P O Stoker mech)

STORIES AND MEMENTOS OF MY TIME SERVED ON HMS 'NASTURTION' (CORVETTE - FLOWER CLASS) ATTACHED TO WESTERN APPROACHES BASED AT LIVERPOOL

My story begins on leaving HMS 'Rodney' after returning to the Royal navy Barracks, Devonport, where I was sent to Middlesborough (Smith Yard) as Advance Party to join a new type of escort vessel which afterwards, turned out to be a Corvette (HMS 'Nasturtion'). Having just come from the battleship HMS 'Rodney', my first reaction when I saw the corvette was to enquire whether this boat was to take out to join the ship allocated to the crew assembled, but the reply I received was 'No, this IS the ship you sail on'! I could hardly believe it, as what I saw looked even smaller than the ferries that crossed the Mersey. When the ship was ready to go to sea and the ship's company all assembled, we set sail to Tobermorey, Scotland for sea trials. After this, we were then attached to 'Captain D - Western Approaches' our run being Liverpool, Iceland, Halifax, Nova Scotia.

Before I start on my story, I would like to tell you that the corvette had no doctor or sick berth attendant, so the 1st Lieutenant said to me 'As you are placed near the medical chest, I will put you in charge of it'. Incidentally, my medical knowledge was absolutely nil, but that didn't seem to be of any consequence! Now, the reason I mention this about the medical chest at this stage, is because it comes into one of my stories later on. I should also mention that the 'Nasturtion' had no canteen on board. This is where my first story begins:-

INTRODUCTION OF A CANTEEN ON HMS 'NASTURTION'

I had reason, whilst in dock in Liverpool, to go into Coopers Stores, in Church Street, for some stores for the ship, and whilst there, the manager of Coopers inquired of me who was the Canteen Manager on our ship. I told him we did not have one and he replied - 'What about you running it and getting your supplies from here?' I asked him what one had to do to go about starting up a canteen, he gave me a form and told me to get the Captain to sign it, and then bring it back to Coopers. I took the form aboard and the Captain signed it without hesitation, and thought it was a damned good idea for the crew. The manager then sent me £12.00 worth of two penny bars of chocolate, which I sold on the Mess Deck as 'Snappy Snacks' to the lads for the total amount of £15.00 thereby making a profit of £3.00. This was the start of my Canteen! As you know, chocolate was rationed during the war years and this little profit I made, gave me great incentive to introduce, if possible, according to what Coopers could offer me, other varieties of snacks as it seemed such a jolly good idea and very popular with the crew. I launched out into small two penny packets of Jacob's biscuits, and from thereon, on arrival in Liverpool after each convoy, I would add several other small items that were offered to me, for sale in the canteen. I said to myself, this is great, as business was booming, my supplies having been exhausted before we were a quarter of the way out to our destination. However, when we arrived in Halifax, I decided to go for it and invest all my takings in a Canadian chocolate 'Noirs Chocolate', a good supply, but now worse was to come, for as we were on convoy back to Liverpool, our ship was damaged and we were ordered to go to Charleston, (South Carolina) for docking and repairs. The further south we went, the hotter and hotter it got, so you can imagine, with having no refrigerator on board, this was indeed a disastrous situation for the chocolate and me. Anyway, on arrival at Charleston, I immediately obtained permission to put the chocolate in the Navy Yard refrigerator, and arranged a lorry to be sent down to the ship to collect it, I may add that the lorry was almost as big as our Corvette!

When the repairs had been carried our and we were ready to leave, my chocolate was brought back again to the ship for inclusion once more in our canteen, but to my utter dismay it all melted, when it was placed in the freezer for return to me, and the whole lot had turned completely white. I had to encourage the lads to buy it at a very cheap rate as it didn't look very presentable. In the end, I had to resort to giving it away, and so ended my dream of making a few bob after investing all my takings in this little venture.

Running the canteen was purely a voluntary task taken on by me and I often wonder, after I left the ship in 1942 to join HMS 'Orion', whether any other subsequent volunteer took the job on.

'BLITZ' JOINS THE CREW OF H.M.S. 'NASTURTION'

Now this story is about a little terrier dog that was a stowaway on our ship and was found one morning after a blitz on Liverpool the previous night. We had set sail for our run and when we were well out, we discovered the terrier dog who had apparently been terrified from the night's happenings. He must have been near Gladstone Dock and ambled up the gangway onto our ship. However, no way could we turn about to land him in Liverpool, so we set sail with him on board and called him the appropriate name of 'BLITZ'. He became a real ship's mascot and a great pet to the company. He ate the same food as the lads, sausage and chips, eggs, etc, as there certainly was not any dog food on board. He soon settled into his new abode and way of life, and when rough seas were encountered, Blitz always knew to get between the stanchions to anchor himself safely.

Whilst in Charleston, Blitz must have taken it upon himself to take a trip ashore, and caused quite a lot of concern when he didn't return to the ship. The lads were anxious, wondering what had happened to him, as we were due to sail in a short while. If I remember rightly, it was printed in the local paper 'Sailors refuse to sail without their dog'. He caused quite a stir, and then happily quite soon after, Blitz returned to his ship quite unharmed and looking O.K. after his trip ashore.

On our return to Liverpool, Kenny, our ASDIC operator, took Blitz to his own home as a family pet, and so that was the end of Blitz's Sea Dog Legs!

THE MEDICAL CHEST

One Christmas day we were sailing up the Gulf of Mexico to Mobile, Alabama and, as I mentioned earlier, I was put in charge of the medical chest. Now in the Navy at that time, we were all issued, every day with a tot of rum which was the Naval tradition then; whether it still exists I do not know. However, as I said, it was Christmas Day and it was decided that we should have an extra drink, if possible, to celebrate the festive season the best we could - but how? that was the question! A decision was made that we should check the medical chest to see if there was anything there that could be conjured up for a drink, as we knew it contained a bottle of pure alcohol. I mentioned this to the cook and asked him if he had any ideas of what we could do with it, and he readily said 'just mix it with prune juice and serve it out as punch'. So that is what we did, and later on as we were sailing along in the afternoon, it was announced that anyone who gave a song would get a sipper of the lethal drink. We had many volunteers to do this, and after a few sippers I am afraid the vocabulary of the songs were far from complimentary about certain members of the ships company - enough said!

Although things were very hard during those times, as indeed it was for many thousands of others, we had many humorous situations arising from time to time which gave us an opportunity to have a good laugh together, and certainly keep our spirits and morale going, even though we were living under very cramped, and in rough seas, very uncomfortable conditions, such was the way of life on a Corvette.

THE SINKING OF A U-BOAT BY H.M.S. 'NASTURTION' (Corvette)

Our ship was one of the Flower Class Corvettes and we managed to trail and sink a U-boat submarine. As the Germans surfaced out of her after she was hit, we rescued a very young survivor. I am afraid he got rather rough handling from different members of the crew who had either lost their entire, or several members of their families, and others who had had their homes laid flat by the Luftwaffe planes when they had raided over England.

When the Germans clothing was examined, in his wallet was found a photograph of his parents and family, and then the lads were sympathetic and after he had been issued with dry clothing, he was placed in the officer's bathroom with a watch guard being kept over him. However, the next morning, on inspection of the bathroom he was found to be dead, and so the captain carried out a simple burial service and our survivor was buried at sea.

Above stories told by;
J.W.J.J. Cox - Naval No DLX/21359
Division - Devonport

S.S. WINNIPEG II

In the mid Atlantic in Convoy on the night of 22.10.42, we were torpedoed by a German U-boat. The sea was very rough and it was a very hard job for the French corvette to pick us up.

After several days we were put ashore at St. Johns, Newfoundland. Then after a few weeks we were transferred to Halifax, Nova Scotia by ship. It should have only taken hours but so many ships were having a bad time outside Halifax that it took us over a week.

We were very well treated by the people of Halifax. The local radio station took some of us into the studio, we thought we were going to send a message home but instead it was only to sing Christmas carols for their programme.

After a couple more months we were put on the S.S.'Andes' for the voyage home.

I was also on the 'Duchess of Bedford' at the invasion in Sicilly.

At the end of the hostilities I was given four medals:

The Atlantic Star
The Italy Star
1939-1945 Star
War Medal

L.J. Cundle

H.M.S. WOLFE

I served on the battleship 'Malaya' on Malta convoys for 18 months from 1941-42 and then on the battleship 'Valiant' with the British American South Pacific Fleet based on Trincomalle in Ceylon for a period of 2 years.

My first ship on the outbreak of war in 1939 was the Armed Merchant Ship (AMC) - HMS 'Wolfe' which was formerly the liner 'Montrose' which sailed under the Cunard flag before the commencement of the war. Based at Greenock, we were assigned to contraband patrol on the Denmark straights and around the Arctic Circle.

South American Nations and indeed the U.S. were neutral and it was common knowledge that cargo ships were carrying contraband to Norwegian ports - a country which fell to the Germans in 1940. To reach these Norwegian ports, ships from South American ports could not take the usual trade routes with the result that they had to sail up the East coast of America, and then through the Denmark Straights across the Arctic Circle and so into Norway.

We had many successful trips up there in the frozen wastes and although we made many captures, our biggest enemy were the elements. Very often our guns were completely frozen - as well as the crew I might add!

My first experience of Atlantic duties was late in 1940 when we were assigned to escort a large convoy from Nova Scotia to the United Kingdom. On leaving the port we found ourselves fogbound off the banks of Newfoundland. Surprisingly, we reached the U. K. ports without incident. Our next assignment was to pick a convoy up off Freetown, West Africa, but somewhere in the Bay of Biscay we were attacked by a Focke Wulf Condor, a long range German bomber out of Brest in France. It was just after darkness had fallen when he flew along our ships length from stern to stem, dropping four 500 lb bombs in quick succession, the first one fell in our wake harmlessly, the second bomb hit us on the boat deck but fortunately, it failed to explode and rolled over the side with the aid of the boy bugler and the navigator who levered it into the sea with a spare piece of wood. The boy bugler, incidentally, was the youngest crew member on board and no more than 18 years old.

Having sustained some damage to our upper deck, we were recalled to the United Kingdom. After repairs were completed, we returned to Northern Patrol in the Arctic and on our first trip back we dropped anchor in a fjord in Iceland where a little further away we noticed the battleship HMS 'Hood'. We were not aware of it at the time, but we sensed something on a large scale was about to take place and indeed it did, for the German battleship 'Bismark', it transpired, was in the Atlantic, ready to wreak havoc on our ships.

I remember asking permission if I could pay a short visit to HMS 'Hood' as I had many shipmates on there that I served with pre-war. My request was granted and after saying goodbye to them on the mess deck, sometime later fate took a hand.

The rest is history, HMS 'Hood' came into contact with the 'Bismark', with a shell from the German warship striking the magazine with the result that the 'Hood' was blown to smithereens with two survivors out of a total of 2,000 crew. As we were in the vicinity of the action at that time, and armed with only 6" guns, our captain cleared low deck to inform us that 'they who fight and run away, live to fight another day'.

We immediately headed down the South Atlantic, finally docking in Hamilton, Bermuda. It was there that I left the 'Wolfe' having been drafted ashore to HMS 'Malbar', a small barracks high up on Bermuda.

I was completely mystified as to what I was doing there, when one morning, all was revealed. There, in the Bay of Bermuda, was a large convoy of some 60 oil tankers which had arrived from the Persian Gulf, bound for the U.K.

Later on that day, I was summoned with some haste to pack my kitbag and hammock and transported to the harbour, from whence I was taken out in a small boat and placed on board a Norwegian oil tanker called 'Belinda'.

On my arrival on board I was immediately sent for by the Captain and all was then revealed, when in his broken English, he explained to me that they had some guns installed, namely 2.4.5 low angle and 4 Hotchkiss anti-aircraft and he went on to say that it was my task to train the ships crew how to use them.

As I held a 1st class gunnery rate I decided that this would not be a problem. Then I discovered that none of them spoke any English, so therefore it was a case of going through the actions instead of explaining by word of mouth.

Fortunately, for the first 4 weeks of our 6 week journey to the U.K., the weather was really foul with mountainous seas, which meant a certain degree of safety as no U-boat could operate in such weather.

The rest of our journey was uneventful I'm glad to say, and on arrival at Stanlow Oil Terminal, (and with my girl friend who I was engaged to, being a native of Liverpool, and who I eventually married in 1942 and celebrated our Golden Wedding in 1992,) I had a few days unofficial leave before reporting to the Liver Buildings and returning to the R.N. Barracks, Portsmouth with sad memories of my former shipmates who gave the ultimate sacrifice on HMS 'Hood'.

Mr. J. F. Cunningham

THE ONE GALLON BOTTLE OF AMMONIA ACID THAT SAVED MY LIFE IN WORLD WAR TWO

On the 7th January, 1942 I sailed out of Gladstone Dock on the M.V. Emile Franquie', a Belgian cargo ship bound for the west - the U.S.A. or Canada. We met up with our convoy at the mouth of the River Clyde. Our ten day crossing of the Atlantic had begun. On 10th January we ran into a storm which was to last for five days with the eighty five to one hundred m.p.h. winds making waves between thirty and fifty feet high. During a very bad spell, the chief steward had gone down below to the store room to get a one gallon bottle of ammonia and called me down to take it up top. On reaching the top of the companionway steps, the ship keeled over very suddenly, causing me to fall and drop the bottle down into the store gangway. You can guess what happened to the chief steward and his fight against the ammonia fumes. Gasping for air and with eyes streaming with tears, he arrived in the dining room saying I had dropped the bottle on purpose. Things between us seemed to be very cool from that day on and he told me, 'Don't ask to sign on again if we reach Liverpool safely'. I took him at his word and left the ship when we arrived back in Liverpool late in February, 1942. We had loaded war aid from Canada in Halifax, Nova Scotia, and St John's, Newfoundland during our stay across the Atlantic.

I joined the M.V. 'Leopoldville', the flag ship of the Belgian fleet and on returning to the United Kingdom in November 1942 I was informed that the 'Emile Franquie' had been lost with all hands due to enemy action in the Atlantic on her next voyage from Liverpool in 1942.

I myself saw further service on the 'Highland Brigade', 'Empress of Scotland', 'Louise Pasteur', 'Reina del Pacifico', a victory ship, 'Empire Pride' and a Royal Navy ship on T124 duty. Now in my sixty eighth year, as I sit writing this, I am thankful to God for dropping that bottle of ammonia acid, which I can assure you was accidental!

Eugene Owen Finnan

THE END OF A U-BOAT

In 1941, I was the Leading Signalman aboard HMS 'Wanderer' escorting an HX convoy of about forty ships. One of these was a C.A.M. ship, the 'Maplin', which was an ex-banana boat, fitted with a catapult which fired a Hurricane fighter. Some days out of Liverpool we were shadowed by a Focke Wolf Condor, which passed to and fro across the path of the convoy calling up the U-boats to intercept us. It was not long before the 'Maplin' launched its fighter with a loud bang and the fighter shot forward; for a moment it looked as though it would hit the water but then it lifted up and streaked between the lines of ships before climbing and disappearing into cloud.

The radio transmitter speaker on the bridge was switched on and the pilot's voice came in loud and clear, 'Have sighted target and am attacking from astern.' Then came the rattle of machine guns and the pilot's excited voice, 'he is going down and I am returning to convoy'.

Some minutes later he appeared over the convoy and did a 'victory roll,. He called out that he was unable to parachute and would land as close to us as possible. We steered a straight course, and down he came in a shallow dive, went into the drink and disappeared. For a moment we thought he was lost; however he bobbed up and the boat we had dropped picked him up. At that moment a U-boat surfaced dead ahead of us so we had to leave the boat to attack the submarine, which had immediately dived again. It was some time before we were able to return to recover the boat. The pilot was dried out and warmed up with a few tots before coming up to the bridge. His name was Flight Lieutenant Everett and he had ridden 'Gregalach' to victory in an Aintree Grand National. I was sad to read some time later that this brave man drowned in the Irish Sea whilst ferrying an aircraft across.

G.S. Gaskin - HMS 'Wanderer' 1940-42

ABANDON SHIP

I first encountered real enemy action at sea in November 1940 when I was an ordinary seaman on the SS 'Fabian' bound for Cape Town, South Africa. After about three weeks at sea, we were torpedoed and sunk by a German U-boat. While we were struggling to abandon ship the submarine surfaced and helped us with some first aid and also apologised for causing us to lose six men! As we had a gun on board, the U-boat had assumed that we would have fired if they had not. The Germans told us we wouldn't be adrift for long as we were in a busy shipping lane and, sure enough, we were picked up three days later by the 'British Statesman' and landed in Freetown, West Africa.

After that experience I had many trips to different parts of the world including the Middle East, U.S.A. and the Caribbean. In December 1942 I suffered a fractured patella during a spell of bad weather and spent some time in hospital and rest-camp in Trinidad.

In March 1943 I was sailing in convoy from New York aboard a Norwegian whaler, the 'Sven Foyne', when we struck an iceberg after a week at sea. We remained afloat for over two days waiting for tugs to come from Reykjavik, Iceland, but we finally had to abandon her; some in boats and some, like myself, taken aboard the American coastguard cutter 'Modoc' and landed in St John's, Newfoundland. I believe that fifty five men were lost in this incident. I am not sure exactly how, as I don't think anyone was injured in the collision but it was extremely cold - nothing but a sea of ice.

After a spell in Halifax, Nova Scotia, I joined a Danish ship SS 'Amerika', and in April 1943 we sailed in convoy carrying a number of Canadian Air Force personnel and general cargo (sacks of flour). We had only been at sea for a few days when we were torpedoed at nine o'clock at night. The ship immediately listed to port. As the crew's quarters were aft we had to make our way midships to the lifeboats which were swinging inwards because of the heavy list. It was not pleasant to contemplate having to launch lifeboats in the dark, either with or against a list. Making my way from aft to midships I decided to go the unorthodox way along the low side (port), The rails were partly in the water and I was washed backwards once but I eventually reached the one stairway connecting to the boat deck. Some of the lads going along the high side of the ship (starboard) were not so lucky and were lost or injured. Despite difficulties because of the list, a few of us eventually managed to get the port lifeboat away and we picked up a woman from the lower deck - a stewardess or ship's doctor, I think. I remember seeing some Air Force lads standing by the bulkhead and someone shouting to them 'You'll be picked up later'. Some were rescued after being found floating on sacks of flour but eighty eight were lost from that ship. I was fortunate to picked up by the corvette HMS 'Asphodel' and put ashore in Scotland.

James ('Mick') Gibbons

TANKER W.B. WALKER

At the outbreak of World War II I had already completed two years of my seagoing days, I immediately applied to join the Royal Navy but I was told that I was already doing a responsible service and they could not accept me.

The War at Sea was very traumatic, at the end of your watch we just climbed into our bunks fully dressed.

New years Day 1941 - I was at sea aboard a tanker named 'W B Walker', an Anglo-American oil tanker. We had left Trinidad with our cargo of Benzine and aviation spirit and had sailed to St John's, Newfoundland in order to join a convoy bound for the UK. The convoy consisted of thirteen ships, including ourselves. Our escort consisted of one destroyer and two armed trawlers. We assembled in three lines, several hundred yards apart, with the destroyers ahead and two trawlers on either side. The speed of the convoy, as was in all convoys, was governed by the maximum speed of the slowest ship which was approximately 10 knots.

It was one o'clock in the morning of 29.1.1941, it was full moon and I was half way through my trick at the wheel, we were about four hundred miles from the Irish coast when we ran into the Wolf Pack, they came up between the lines of ships. When the alarm was raised, the order came to disperse at full speed, but in the meantime four ships had been torpedoed, and I began to sweat. The dreaded moment came and the torpedo struck us amidships. The main mast crashed down across the flying bridge and the binnacle, which houses the compass that I had been steering by, tumbled over on it's side. I froze to the wheel waiting to meet my creator, because, with the cargo we were carrying, it only required a spark. Hearing the captain screaming to abandon ship brought me to my senses. There was a mad scramble for the lifeboats which we lowered, boarded, and began to row away from the ship, but by this time most of us were being affected by the fumes of ruptured tanks. Four crew members, including the 'Bosun' were killed. The bosun, who survived the explosion, and who was in another lifeboat, drowned when being overcome by fumes, slipped over the edge of the lifeboat.

Sometime later, we were picked up by the destroyer and soon after transferred to a trawler. All that night the destroyer and trawlers steamed at speed around the area dropping depth charges and firing star shells, which proved quite unnerving to us survivors who were battened down below decks.

However, we survived the night and next morning when we came on deck, we were all amazed to find that the tanker was still afloat with a huge hole in her side. After circling the tanker for more than an hour, it was decided by the officers that an attempt should be made to salvage her. A radio message was sent requesting assistance of a deep sea tug. In the meantime, the first mate of the tanker asked for volunteers to return to the ship in order to prepare her for towing. Six of the tankers crew, including myself, elected to do so. One of the ships lifeboats was used for us to row the two or three hundred yards which separated the two ships. As we neared the tanker, a plane appeared and we held our breath until we realised it was a Sunderland Flying Boat. We reached the tanker, tied up the lifeboat to the tankers rail and scrambled aboard. At this point, I must mention that the sea was quite rough with a heavy swell. We made our way to the foredeck, it took us some time to haul up the heavy towing lines from the forepeak and prepare the anchor cable, We had just finished this very hard work when, with a great screaming and rending of steel plates, the tanker broke her back, rupturing fresh tanks with the resulting escape of fumes. Needless to say, salvage was now out of the question and we very quickly got back to the lifeboat and returned to the trawler, we saw that the tanker had broken in two and the two halves were still floating some distance apart. We heard later that the tanker had been sunk by shellfire from the destroyer in order to prevent it becoming a hazard to shipping.

Several days later, we were landed at Londonderry, and from there to Greenock, Scotland where I boarded a train for Liverpool. As I was walking through Lime Street Station, a woman stopped me and without saying anything, handed me a white feather, not realising the significance of this, I thanked her and put it in my pocket. When I arrived home, after all the hugs and kisses, I showed the feather to my mother and told her of the incident at the station, needless to say, my dad and I had to restrain her from putting on her hat and coat and taking a tram to the station to try to find this woman.

James Griffiths

A MEMORY OF THE BATTLE OF THE ATLANTIC

One day, I was at the docks in Gibraltar, waiting for the shore engineers to repair the engine of our old oil-tanker, 'British Freedom'. This was the fourth time we had encountered engine trouble while sailing. As we waited, we noticed a lot of excited people heading towards the harbour where a British corvette, the 'Mayflower' was escorting a captured U-boat into port. It received a rousing welcome with crowds cheering and clapping and ships hooters blaring.

Two days later the 'Mayflower' escorted the 'British Freedom' through the straights of Gibraltar on a voyage to Curacao, a Dutch island in the Caribbean, to pick up a cargo of fuel oil. We sailed past the Canary Isles and three or four days later broke down again! The ship's engineers had to fit new cylinder linings in the engines. This took about twelve hours and meanwhile, we were sitting targets. We hoped and prayed that we wouldn't be spotted by enemy aircraft or U-boats.

Finally, we arrived at Curacao and the shore engineers once again set to work on our engines. After we had taken on our cargo, we set sail for Sydney, Cape Breton Island in Nova Scotia where there was a large enclosed bay which was ideal for convoys to assemble. As the convoy left the bay we raised our anchor in order to proceed but the engine failed to start! Yet again we had to call on the services of the shore engineers.

At last we were able to leave Sydney and follow the convoy. We caught up with it and got in line taking an inside position because we were carrying an important cargo. All ships with dangerous or valuable cargoes did this for added protection.

As the convoy sailed on towards North Shields, an enormous explosion suddenly broke the calm. The ship on our left had been hit by a torpedo and very quickly fire enveloped the deck from bow to stern. I was at the helm of my ship and looked at the inferno in horror and a great sadness overcame me; I thought there would be no survivors. On my ship, I could hear a seventeen year old boy in a very distressed state because his father was the Captain of the ship that was sinking and his thoughts were the same as mine.

Some years later, I had just finished my shore leave and was on my way to the 'Seaman's Pool' at the Pier Head to get shipped out again, when I suddenly bumped into the young lad who had been on the 'British Freedom' with me. He had grown into a tall young man and had a big smile on his face. I asked him how he was and he astonished me by saying 'I am off to London to see my father receive his medals; he is being decorated today'. Tears of joy welled in my eyes. I was so happy and proud for him. Only the five crew members on the bridge of his father's ship had survived that terrible fire to be picked up by the rescue ship. Sad to say all the other hands perished.

I sailed on about eight crossings of the North Atlantic run and received my 'Atlantic Star' personally but many families received medals on behalf of loved ones who had bravely died for their country.

Harold Goodier

THE LACONIA INCIDENT

I first went to sea as a cabin boy in 1936 with the John Holt Line. I was discharged from the Merchant Navy as a result of shell shock in 1943, and was a dock worker from then until 1945. I then worked as a plasterer until my retirement. I was one of eight children and was born in Lloyd Street, Everton.

In 1940, I sailed to Canada on the SS 'Beatus', six thousand tons, belonging to Seigers of Cardiff Ltd. We left Halifax, Nova Scotia, in a convoy of thirty two ships on October 18th, 1940. 'Beatus' was carrying a cargo of steel and pit props.

While sailing at six knots, the convoy was attacked by U-boats, the 'Fiscus' was sunk and the 'Beatus' was hit by torpedoes. We were rescued by HMS 'Bluebell', a corvette. This attack was believed to be the first by U-boats operating in a 'Wolf Pack'.

I arrived eventually at Greenock and stayed overnight on the SS 'Cree Kirk' before continuing homeward.

In June 1942 I joined the SS 'Laconia' carrying allied troops to North Africa. We were returning through the Atlantic with two thousand Italian prisoners of war when we were torpedoed and sunk by a U-boat, commanded by Lieutenant-Commander Werner Hartenstein (U156). The U-boat surfaced and took the lifeboats in tow, and a message was sent that no rescue ships would be attacked. Help was received from La Gloire. I, and my comrades were interned in Casablanca for eight weeks, finally being liberated by the U.S. Army. I was sent to the U.S.A. and repatriated soon afterwards.

Frank Holding

IN BATTLE WITH SS 'ARDEOLA'

In October, 1942 we loaded up, mainly with foodstuffs, in Coberg Dock, on SS 'Ardeola'. Our normal trip was Lisbon to Gibraltar, however, firstly we proceeded up to Scotland to join a convoy and a few days later, when it was assembled, we knew instantly it was no ordinary trip as the number of escorts was unbelievable.

Halfway through the trip, the deck hands began painting the ship in neutral colours and carpenters altered the outline with wood and canvas.

As was the usual practice, we passed Gibraltar at night. We went near to Algiers with the invasion fleet, for by this time we realised that's what it was, and our ship and another ran along the coast. We were trying to get to Malta under cover of darkness. French flags were hung over the side, and we changed our name to SS 'G.G. Lampeene' registered in Marseilles. It wasn't long before bombers from Sicily were on their way to bomb the invasion fleet. They came at us below mast height, looked at us and carried on.

We got to within 24 hours of Malta when we were shelled by French coastal guns at Bizerte. Both crews were then taken prisoner of war and transferred to a POW camp where we met approximately 360 other merchant seamen, survivors at earlier Malta convoys. Some had even been there three years: When I think only one ship got through, SS 'Port Chalmers'; we were in a very tight spot. Montgomery was chasing the Africa Corps on top of us from the East, and the Germans had landed in Tunisia, so we were between the two.

After a while, the French camp commandant marched us all out. After the Axis Armistice Commission left, he commanded a freight train to take us into the mountains, where we all hid for a while near some old salt mines. Eventually, we went to a small railhead called Coustantine, and I think an American Army officer put us on a train for Algiers, where we boarded the SS 'Orontes' for England, arriving home a few days before Christmas 1942.

It was such a relief to be home. My brother still has the telegram from the War Office telling my mother her two sons were missing at sea, but may be prisoners of war. The thing which is hard to believe is that no-one received a penny compensation as the Ministry said we were not POW's, but political prisoners.

C Kennedy

P.S. When we arrived at Algiers, the French ship SS 'G G Lapeene' was still in harbour, our ship looked nothing like her, she had three masts, very unusual in steam ships - so much for British Intelligence!

A UNIQUE EXPERIENCE

I was working in the Photographic section at Luqa on 28 September 1941, as usual, when the duty orderly room runner came to the section with instruction. I had to go to my barrack block, pack all my gear, and be outside the orderly room in two hours ready for return to the UK. I did not require a second telling and duly arrived back at HQ together with other bods who had received the same instruction. We boarded the transport which took us down to Custom House Jetty where we witnessed the arrival of a convoy. A flat barge came alongside which took us across Grand Harbour, to where a large naval vessel was tied up. It turned out to be the cruiser HMS 'Kenya'. Whilst we were boarding for'ard, we could see other bods disembarking aft. We were detailed to our messdecks, mine was the hangar, the 'Walrus' having been lashed down on deck. All this time the derricks and dockside cranes had been working full blast, when all the activities had finished, we slipped our moorings and headed out of the harbour to anchor a few miles off shore. It was then that we were instructed to parade on the for'ard deck. When we had fallen in, we were told that as the ship was being used to transport troops, she did not have a full complement of Royal Marines on board, which meant that we would have to help man the ship during 'Action Stations'. Aircrews and armourers were called for first, they were detailed to man the light armament. then volunteers were called for in numbers ie; five, two, four etc. I waited a while thinking that I was being crafty and that all the best jobs would be last, but not so! Twelve were called for and I, together with others, stepped forward. 'You, you and you', 'A' turret shell room. One of the crew was detailed to show us the way to get to our station. Along the deck we went, through the bulkhead doors, through the hatches, down ladders until we at last arrived at 'A' turret shell room, below 'A' turret. Below the water line and right at the sharp end! not a very nice place to be with all the six inch shells stacked around the racks. Our duty was to keep the outer turntable filled with shells, this was controlled by a large wheel which was turned by one of the naval bods so that which ever way the opening for the shell hoist was turned, shells would be opposite to it, so that the person putting the shells into the hoist had only to reach a short distance.

We returned to the hangar where we had a meal, when darkness fell we were called to 'action stations' and with a darkened ship, we up-anchored and at full speed made a dash through the narrows between Pantalleria and Sicilly, so that we could get clear at daybreak. I cannot recommend the steel room of a shell room as an ideal way to spend the first night on board ship. Apart from the explosive surrounds, it was darned uncomfortable. We did have one or two calls to 'action stations' in the Med. but nothing happened, so it was either shadowing aircraft or just practice to keep us on our toes. One night we were told that we would be in harbour at Gib, by reveille, so we bedded down expecting to see the first glimpse of land since leaving Malta. Day dawned, and rubbing our sleepy eyes we went out on deck expecting to see the massive rock towering above us. But no, there was no sight of land, just an endless expanse of water all around us and we were travelling at some knots. We knew that the navy was good at navigation and could not possible have missed the Rock. There must be some other explanation - there was.

The ships communications came on - it was the Captain speaking - we had in fact, entered the harbour during the night and picked up more passengers. he also told us that when we had arrived in harbour, he had been summoned to the navy HQ and it was reported to him that a U-boat supply ship, escorted by surfaced U-boats was in that sector of the Atlantic. His orders were; 'to search for and destroy'

The old Walrus went off, I am not sure how long it was before it returned with it's Aldis lamp flashing and the order to 'action stations' was sounded, this was it. We closed up, 'A' and 'B' opened up, followed by the after turrets. This went on for a while followed by a brief 'cease fire'. Then we were ordered to load with a different type of shell and in we went again. Our turret had fired a salvo, followed by the after turrets when, suddenly, there was a dull thud followed by a slight vibration to our ship. The naval bod who was by the hoist looked at us and said 'It's either them or us'. suddenly we heard a loud shout from the voice pipe, this was the communication system to the gun turret, the bod on the hoist spoke into it and them put his ear to it. Gradually a smile spread across his face and turning to us he said 'we got it!' It was our turn to cheer, we had struck a blow for Malta - there would be a few less U-boats to attack the convoys.

When we stood down, the Captain once more came on the air to say that he was pleased with the result of our attack, but the sea was much too calm and the crews looked too comfortable in their boats. It appears we had ceased fire to allow the crew to abandon ship.

After the action, HMS 'Kenya' set course for home, eventually we arrived in port at Gourock where, that night we boarded a train for an unknown destination. With blacked out windows, we travelled through the night and eventually arrived at West Kirby PDC., where we stayed for a couple of days for medical and documentation. The camp was not far from my home in Cheshire. With all the excitement of being home I did not get in touch with my mother or sister. My father had been killed at work in 1934, just a few weeks before I went for my RAF and evening class examinations. We were sent on disembarkation leave. I arrived at my local station and the first thing I did was to ring the local telephone exchange where my sister worked as a telephonist, only to be told that she had not long finished her duties for that day and had left for home. So, I ordered a taxi and headed for home. We had gone a couple of miles when I thought I spotted someone who looked like my sister, so I asked the driver to slow down. As we passed by, I could see that it was my sister and I asked the driver to stop a little way ahead. When she came up to us I opened the window and asked if she would like a lift. She thanked me and as the driver opened the door for her to get in, it was only then that she noticed who was on the back seat. Needless to say, she was more than surprised and she told me that only a few days earlier they had posted my Christmas parcel. When we arrived home and before the taxi had properly stopped, she had the door open, was out of the taxi and into the house to tell mother the news. I was home for Christmas.

Since joining the Association, I have made contact with a Royal Marine who was on the upper deck and saw all of the action. He told me that when we went into action, there were a number of U-boats tied up alongside the supply ship. The crews could be seen hurrying along the upper deck making their way to get on board and cast off. He did not think that more than one managed to do this, so when the supply ship blew up, it took with it the U-boats tied up alongside. At the same time as we were carrying out the attack we were dropping depth charges, so perhaps more U-boats 'bit the dust'.

Harry Kirk (ex RAF)

GLAD WHEN THE WAR WAS OVER

After evacuating 300 children from Liverpool to Wellington, New Zealand in April, 1940 on TSS 'Ruahine' we joined a convoy in Halifax and set off homeward bound. All the way back to the U.K. we were attacked by submarines day and night. When we were about seventy miles West of Ireland, German long range planes also joined in. Many of the ships in the convoy were sunk. We had to wear lifejackets all the time, both on and off watch so that we were glad to get into port to have a bath and a change of clothes. I soon found myself on the tanker 'Tornus' which was loaded with aviation fuel. I remember standing by lifeboats both day and night seeing many ships getting sunk all around us. I transferred to the M V 'Darina' on the 20th May 1942, this was hit by two torpedoes and later a submarine surfaced and fired 26 shells at us as we were being taken to the lifeboats. Some crew members were killed by the shrapnel and many others were wounded. We then spent over a week in a lifeboat in appalling weather about 480 miles North East of Bermuda. A Norwegian ship called 'Dagrun' picked us up and landed us in Capetown 30 days later. This ship was bound for Egypt from New York but took a long route around the Cape as the Mediterranean was closed to shipping.

Next, I joined a new ship 'Empire Spenser', a tanker loaded with Benzine from Curacao, in the Dutch West Indies. On the way home, we were torpedoed and set on fire. I managed to get on a raft but not before my hands and feet were blistered with the flames. A rescue ship 'Perth' picked us up and landed us at Greenock. We were rigged out with new clothes and shoes and sent home.

I continued my war on 'British Lady' and our job was to fuel escorts at sea. The convoy was attacked in thick fog and ice just off the coast of

Newfoundland, so we had to put into St John's and await orders. I was also on another tanker 'Empire Cavalier' running from the USA to North Africa.

I was glad when the war ended.

Denis P McAllister - R.164809

TRUST IN GOD AND 'GOOD LUCK'

I still have vivid and endless memories of the Atlantic Battle, recollection of convoys, often with totally inadequate numbers of escorts, battling against hurricane conditions as well as the threat of the enemy. The never-ending rolling and pitching; the huge green seas that washed over the decks and alleyways and made life utterly miserable. On some trips the weather was kinder, but the main threat was still there, and you hoped for a good position in the convoy. As you formed up, you watched anxiously for your number - were you in an outside column? Or, worse still, were you in 'coffin corner' at the rear or were you the 'tail-end Charlie'?

One night in October, 1941, we were in an outward bound convoy to West Africa - destination Far East - carrying ammunition, guns and army equipment, when at about 10.30 pm we heard an explosion and the accompanying underwater thud on the hull. We were up and out in a flash to see that the ship closest to us, on our port beam, had been torpedoed and was on fire from for'ard to aft. We heard the shouts of her Dutch crew and saw them running along the decks, silhouetted against the flames. The ship was the 'Bennekom' and she slowly stopped and drifted astern as the convoy steamed on. You rarely heard any more about such incidents. If you carried ore - either iron or copper pyrites - then the dice were loaded against you because, if the ship was torpedoed, she invariably went straight under, and, unless you happened to be on deck, your chance of survival was very remote. One of my former ships was torpedoed near Gibraltar and only eight were saved; the helmsman just stepped into the sea at the wheelhouse door!

On the other hand, you could sail independently, as we did, totally alone, with no escort, for over six thousand miles, from the U.K. to Uruguay and arrive safely. We carried extra coal bunkers on deck and under the fo'c'sle head so that we didn't have to stop en-route. Water was rationed and the galley pump locked.

The 'Graf Spee' was still smouldering off Montevideo on our first run down but we made if safely both ways - twice! We put our trust in God and 'Good Luck' but other ships were less fortunate and the six years of war claimed many ships and the lives of many brave shipmates.

A McArdle

A TRUE STORY OF MY AUSTRALIAN PRISONER OF WAR FRIEND SNOWY SULLIVAN - 1941-45

In 1941 my ship the SS 'Logician' left Liverpool with 7000 tons of tanks and ammunition for the Greek island of Crete. My ship was sunk by Germans in Crete, and four of my shipmates went down with the ship when it was blown up. I was wounded and taken to hospital, from where I was taken by prison ship to a prisoner of war camp in Germany. The camp was called 'Marlag und Nord'.

We had over 700 merchant navy sailors, from the English, Australian and U.S.A. forces. In 1942 a bunch of Australian prisoners came into the camp. I remember an Australian sailor came into my barracks room, he said to me, pointing to the bunk over mine, 'is this bunk taken, mate'? I told him that it wasn't and that he may take it. That was the first time I ever met Snowy Sullivan; it was November 1942.

He told me that his ship 'Port Brisbane' was sunk by a German submarine and that he was with some of his mates in an open boat for six days, he was then picked up by a German prison ship and taken to Germany. He said his name was Snowy Sullivan and that it was his first trip to sea. He was only sixteen years old. He told me that his father was a Brisbane police sergeant and that all his brothers were in the forces. Before the ship was sunk he was in London, with food and beef for Britain from the Australian people. He then said that he had met a girl in London and when the war was over he was going to go back and marry her and settle down. But Snowy was very weak and had a bad chest.

I was working on a farm and every night he would wait for me to come back to the camp and I would give him some German meat and bread which I got from the farmer. One day I told the farmer all about my friend Snowy and that he was feeling very ill. He told me he would send a letter to the German Commander for permission to let him work with me on the farm for a few months. He was a good worker, but to me there was still something wrong with poor Snowy. Every night I would hear him fighting for his breath.

Then, one day in Summer, all the farmers were picking the potatoes and a German soldier came over and told them that three prisoners had tried to escape; an Australian and two French prisoners. When they told me it was Snowy I just felt sick. They were captured the next day. The three of them gave themselves up. They were dying of hunger.

The commander told the farmer that Snowy must not be allowed out of the camp ever again. Every night Snowy would keep on telling me all about the girl he had met in London. I remember it was May 1943 and I was coming our of the prison chapel and I was looking at Snowy. He was pointing through the barbed wire out at the sunset, 'look Timmy, look at the wonderful sunset'. Every evening he would look at the sun going down over the prison camp. Some of the boys started saying 'what's wrong with Snowy'?

Then, one day I was lying on my bunk and Snowy came over and sat on the end of my bunk and said 'I've got something for you; look, I've written a song; please, I want you to think up a tune. I've called it 'Until the Dawn, My Love'. Now all the boys really did think Snowy has gone mushy.

Then the day I will always remember, 1945 when we were all getting liberated from the camp. Snowy came over to me, 'Goodbye Timmy my 'Pooly' friend, thanks for being a good pal to me'. He then gave me the paper with the song on and said, 'please find a tune for me. I have got your address, I will send you mine from London'. That was the last time I ever saw Snowy Sullivan.

Two years later I went to a prisoner of war reunion for sailors in Liverpool; some of the boys came from Australia; we all had plenty to drink. I asked if they had seen Snowy, and did he marry his girl in London? They told me the story of Snowy. When he returned to London, the girl he was supposed to marry had already married and had a little four year old baby girl. It just broke his heart. On the way back to Brisbane to see his family, he died of T.B.

But I must carry out Snowy's wish. I want the people of Brisbane to help me to donate the song for the merchant seamen and the returned prisoners of war all over Australia.

Timmy McCoy

This song first came to light in a Merchant Navy P.O.W. Camp during the last war, when it was sung by myself and other prisoners. I have put this to music and am dedicating it to my colleagues and their wives.

'UNTIL THE DAWN'

Until the dawn my love
How many moons will shine above
Until I make you mine my love
Do many Bluebirds fly
Across the same old summer sky?
How many lonely nights go by
While I remain alone

How many rivers will flow to the sea
How many times will it rain,
How many dreams will you dream of me
Darling, till we meet again?
Though autumn leaves will fall
Upon the same old garden wall
I know my lonely heart will call,
Until the dawn my love
I know my lonely heart will call,
Until the dawn my love.

Snowy Sullivan

'BLITZ'

This is a story about a very unusual 'chap' who also served in the Battle of the Atlantic. Whilst serving aboard HMS 'Nasturtium', a flower class corvette, we steamed into Liverpool having seen many losses and much heroism, in order to berth at Gladstone Dock. There was the usual big air raid on at the time but by now we had grown quite used to them.

When we had steamed past the 'bar' we discovered a stowaway, a scruffy looking Mongrel dog. We named the dog 'Blitz'.

After a few days ashore, we were then ready to rendezvous with another convoy. We had steamed out past the 'Bar' when we discovered a stowaway, a scruffy looking mongrel dog. We named the dog 'Blitz' assuming he had come aboard in fear of the noise during the air raid. Blitz soon became a big favourite with us all, although it was pathetic watching him trying to get his sea-legs on a corvette in the Atlantic Ocean.

Blitz made many crossings and saw a lot of action. However, after returning at the end of 1942, we were ordered to North Africa for the invasion. Once again Blitz was in action, this time attacked from aircraft - not U-boats. But after we had sailed from Oran, Algeria, I discovered we had lost Blitz for ever. I sometimes wonder if dogs go to the same place as humans - was he put on Captains defaulters and given ninety days in the dog pound for going A.W.O.L.?

T. McDonald

THE BATTLE OF THE BARRANTES SEA
(Captain R.ST.V. Sherbrook D.S.O. R.N.)

This convoy of fourteen ships left Loch Ewe on 22nd December, 1942. It was to have been escorted by seven destroyers, two corvettes, two trawlers and one minesweeper. But one destroyer suffered severe weather damage on the way to Seidisfiord and could not take part, one lost touch between Jay Mayen and Bear Island due to a Gyro failure, the minesweeper, one trawler and two merchant ships became detached in a gale the next day.

AT 08.30 on New Years Eve therefore, the situation was as follows;

The convoy now reduced to 12 ships, was on an Easterly course, about 220' NNW of the Kole Inlet and 13' South of its ordered route. The escort still in company of H.M. destroyers 'Onslow' (Captain R. St. V. Sherbrook D.S.O. R.N. Captain (D) 17th Destroyers Flotilla).'Obedient' (E.L. Solater D.S.O. RN) 'Orwell' (Lt Commander N.H.G.Austen D.S.O. RN), 'Achetes' (Lt Commander L.A. Sayers RNR), 'Hyderabad' (Lt S.C.B. Hickman D.S.O. RNR and HMS Trawler 'Northern Gem' (Skipper Lt W.J. Mullender R.D. RNR).

Some 35' to the Northward was HM trawler 'Vizalma' (Temporarily Lt J.R. Anglebeock R.N.V.R.) with one merchant ship in company, and about 15' to the North Eastward was HMS 'Bramble' (Commander H.T. Rust, D.S.O. RN). Rear Admiral R.L. Burnett C.B., O.B.E. (Rear Admiral Home Fleet Destroyers). Flying his flag in HMS 'Sheffield'. Captain a. W. Clarke, RN) with HMS 'Jamaica' (Captain J.L. Storey RN). In company was about 25' North of the convoy and 10' South of the 'Vizalma'. None of these four groups knew each others relative position, and there was one other straggler in the vicinity.

Reports had been received of D/F bearings of the one U-boat well ahead of the convoy, one U-boat well to the Southward and an enemy destroyer off North Cape. A suspected U-boat had been reported and attacked without success the evening before, but there was otherwise no indication that the enemy was at sea, or even aware of the passage of the convoy.

The visibility in the twilight was about 7' to the Northward and 10' to the Southward. The sky was mostly covered with low cloud, wind WNW force 3, sea slight with no swell. There was 16' of frost and ice on all the ships.

The 'Hyderabad', on the starboard of the convoy, sighted two destroyers (later to be seen three) bearing 180' at 08.20. She thought they were Russian destroyers in to reinforce the escort and did not report them, but they were sighted and reported soon afterwards by the 'Obdurate' stationed on the starboard beam of the convoy. She closed them at best speed and they returned to the North Westward, across the stern of the convoy, opening fire at 09.30 on the 'Obdurate', who retired on the convoy. Captain (D) 17 from ahead, altered down the port side of the convoy and ordered the destroyers to concentrate while the 'Orwell', 'Obedient' and 'Obdurate' were moving to comply, the 'Achetes, whose station was on the port quarter started to lay a smoke screen to cover the convoy, which made an emergency turn to 135' before the other destroyers had joined, the 'Onslow' sighted a large ship to the North

Westward, coming towards her at high speed. This was the German cruiser 'Hipper'. she turned East and opened fire on 'Achetes', who was very conspicuous because of her smoke screen. The 'Onslow' immediately attacked and opened fire at the 'Hipper' at 09.00 and turned on course as she did so to keep between the 'Hipper' and the convoy; the other three 'O' class destroyers 'Obedient', 'Obdurate' and 'Orwell' were coming up to join 'Onslow' in the attack, the 'Hipper' then turned Northwards under a smoke screen firing as she did so. The 'Onslow' was badly damaged and Captain Sherbrook badly injured.

During this action, before he was injured, Captain (D) 17 had concluded that the enemy was unwilling to face the risk of a torpedo attack by our destroyers. He had then detached 'Obedient' and 'Obdurate' to close the convoy and increase its protection against more attacks, with Captain (D) Sherbrook now injured and 'Onslow' damaged, the Commanding Officer (HMS 'Obedient') - Captain Kinlock, had taken command.

Since the Commanding Officer HMS 'Obedient' had taken command and the 'Hipper' had been driven off, the close escort had been shepherding the convoy to the south. Several enemy ships had been reported but none of these attacked and it is possible that the reports were mistaken. The 'Obedient', 'Orwell' and 'Obdurate' were concentrated between the convoy and the enemy. The 'Onslow' was stationed at the head of the convoy and the 'Achetes reported that she was holed forward and her speed reduced to 15 knots. She had been covering the convoy with smoke, (with the utmost coolness and efficiency) since the start of the action and had sustained this damage from a near miss at about 09.45.

Unfortunately, she again became the first target of the attacking heavy unit the pocket battleship 'Lutzow', the 'Hipper' and six Narvick class destroyers, her bridge was hit , her commanding officer - Captain Johns killed, and considerable damage to the boiler room and other parts of the ship was done.

In spite of all this, 'Achetes' continued to screen the convoy with smoke for another hour and forty minutes, until, compelled at 13.00 hrs to send out a signal to the trawler 'Northern Gem' to come to her assistance as she was now on her side. The survivors were now on the ships side as the 'Northern Gem' came up to the 'Achetes', she started to sink, bows first. The loss of this destroyer and so many of her excellent company after the outstanding work she had done is most deeply regretted. 81 survivors were picked up.

The enemy ship, after damaging 'Achetes' had been engaging the remaining three destroyers, trying to break through to the convoy; she managed to put 'Obedient's' W/T out of action, and the 'Obdurate' was ordered to assume command, but apart from this she had no success while several hits were claimed on her. Two destroyers which followed her took no part in the action. She disappeared to the North Westwards at 11.30. Twice more during the next forty minutes an enemy heavy ship approached the convoy but each time she was driven off by the escort.

On the first of these occasions, the shell splashes are reported to have been larger than any others seen that day, and it seems probable that these two attacks, at any rate, were made by the 'Lutzow'. Finally, this ship, whoever she was, also withdrew to the North Westward.

The heavy cruisers 'Sheffield' and 'Jamaica' had joined with the escort and maintained touch with the heavy German ships until 13.45 hrs by which time it was established that beyond all doubt they were retiring back towards base. Minor damage was sustained, but no casualties. The cruisers returned to cover the convoy. Later on that evening, the 'Obedient' and 'Obdurate' located the 'Northern Gem' who told the ships that she had 81 survivors on board from the 'Achetes' which had sunk. The close escort, who were unaware that the enemy had finally left, spent an anxious night, but there were no further attacks and the convoy arrived complete at Kola Inlet. 'Obedient' and 'Obdurate' escorted 'Northern Gem' to the Murmansk.

The conduct of all officers and men of the escort covering forces throughout this successful action against greatly superior forces, was in accordance with the traditions of the service. That an enemy force of at least one pocket battleship, one heavy cruiser and six destroyers, with all the advantage of surprise and concentration, should be held off for four hours by five destroyers and driven from the area by two cruisers, without any loss to the convoy, is most creditable and satisfactory.

James J McHugh

SOUL DESTROYING CONVOYS TO RUSSIA AND MALTA

It only seems like yesterday since I was sailing out of Liverpool, on a regular basis crossing and re-crossing the North Atlantic.

Many days at sea in Winter, in some of the worst North Atlantic weather imaginable, skirting Iceland and Greenland. These memories have still refused to go away. In the circumstances, it was a wonder a lot more ships were not lost by accident, especially at night with all ships blacked out, in the struggle of keeping station in vile weather in convoy. Even so, as happened a number of times, the weather won and the convoy had to scatter, it was then each ship for itself, later making a further convoy rendezvous, if, and when the weather abated.

The Merchant Navy men were never ones to 'crow', they just did their job and the satisfaction was getting their cargo into port intact and then enjoying their few days leave before sailing once again.

They were a breed of men who did a vital job of work, when it was required, with a minimum of fuss, despite, when in the early years of the war, convoy escorts were scarce and convoys were subjected to heavy U-boat attacks and suffered appalling losses due to lack of escort vessels and the trained men to man them. I blame this situation on the political outlook of the British governments of the 30's, which proved to be abysmal.

Despite Germany's declared re-arming and avowed intention to seek revenge over their defeat in 1918, (Hitler even published a book to this effect) all our ruling governments in the 30's, through complacency or incompetence, or both, chose to ignore this threat until it was too late.

No human being should have been expected to face the unequal struggle the M.N. found itself facing. The M.N. was not even a fighting service, but a civilian floating means of transportation.

However, despite the odds stacked against them, they never flinched. The convoys to Russia and Malta were especially soul destroying, but they pushed on, despite on occasion, losing most of their convoy.

They went to all points of the compass they were asked to go. Very many of these sailors lost their lives to enemy action and have no known grave. Eventually, due to intensive allied building of escort vessels and trained crews to man them, the U-boat menace was overcome, but what a struggle it had been.

Roy H Melbourne

THE 'GLOUCESTER CASTLE'

The 'Gloucester Castle' set sail from Birkenhead bound for South Africa on 2 June 1942. The ship was a coal burner aged about 36 or 37 years. As we drew nearer to Freetown the convoy began to break up. Captain Rose decided that we would carry on alone to Capetown rather than wait for another convoy. This decision was made based on the belief that it would be safe because we were out of the U-boat area. Yet as we carried on in the waters just off the West Coast of Africa, it became clear that we were not safe at all from enemy fire.

At 6p.m. on 15 July 1942 disaster struck in the form of a German raider. It seemed to me as if the whole world had opened up into a fire of machine guns and shells. On board we had about 40 gallon drums of aeroplane dope which were stacked outside the crew's entrance to accommodation down below. Our first thought when it all caught fire was that maybe the ammunition locker had caught fire.

As I threaded my way between the flames, which were not yet all over the deck, I realised that the water had found its way into the accommodation on the saloon deck. I didn't realise at this time that the ship was sinking. By this time, all the alarms were sounding, having been activated by the turning upside down of the lights. As I emerged on the deck, I realised that all the lifeboats had been smashed into pieces of wood. We managed to find a boat and lowered it down into the water, firstly throwing into it our friend Dave Jones, who had broken a leg.

One particularly vivid memory from this incident is of the stewardess. There was a rope ladder which led down to the boat, but the stewardess and an old lady passenger couldn't make it down into the boat. So the stewardess turned to the old lady and said 'Come with me back to my cabin and we'll talk to God'.

As I stood on the deck the whole ship went down. I held my breath, I could feel my lungs bursting so I began to take in sea water which seemed to ease the pain in my chest. Gradually the blackness before my eyes changed to grey and I realised that I was coming up to the surface. Soon I heard a voice shouting and realised that I had come up near that lifeboat into which we had thrown Davy Jones. We managed to pull a few people out of the water, but as we did this we became aware of a huge ship alongside us.

The ship had gone down in four minutes and when the Germans realised that we were a passenger carrying ship they jumped in to help rescue the women and children. Two women and two boys aged about 10 and 14 were pulled up onto the German ship.

When we were all on board, the raider rushed away for fear that any merchant might spot them. We were now prisoners of war on board a ship which was to sink 5 or 6 other ships as well as collecting stragglers out of the water as a means to identify the ship. The Germans had to get away as quickly as possible from a sinking ship because the ship would send out an international call for 'Raider' 'R.R.R.' followed by the ships position. In order to prevent this the German captain would want to wipe out the radio shack and the masts.

We knew which way we were heading because the British navigators could determine the ship's course from the sun. We were heading towards the Germans' allies in the Far East.

On board we even hatched a plot to grab the bridge from the German guards as the ladies in the cabin down below gave us a map telling us their positions on the ship. We were going to grab the guards who had stick grenades, which we were most frightened of. However, one of the Yankee seamen gave us away tipping them off and so after that conditions were much stricter and we were not allowed on deck any longer.

When we came ashore in Japan, at Osaka, we were made to work on board for about two weeks whilst our fate was decided. Eventually the Japanese came on board and took over immediately. We were marched through the streets to the railway station. The white men were put first, then the black men, after them the Chinese and lastly the women and children. We demanded that the women and children march with us but this request was brutally denied as they set about us with rifles used as beating sticks, until we marched to their orders. We were put into cattle trucks and taken to the camp at Osaka.

We were addressed in Japanese, but there was some interpretation. Eventually we got our first meal for 12-18 hours, which consisted of a rice ball. For the next three and a half years the daily meal was such, a rice ball, although on Sunday a little piece of fish was chopped into it. Red Cross parcels did arrive at the camp but the benefits were enjoyed by the guards. We were sent out in working parties and the civilians treated us well, we were delivered by a guard and left there. But we couldn't escape as our faces would be noticed too quickly in the streets. In order to keep going, we created various strategies by which we could steal food.

A bond of friendship did develop between us and some of the civilians. One lady I remember particularly we used to call Mamasan. One day she called me over and said 'Morris-san, the Emperor is making a speech today'. Indeed at 12.00pm we were marched to one end of the crowd and there the Emperor was ready to announce the end of the war.

Indeed she was right, the next day we awoke to new circumstances as we realised that the ever present guards were gone. We walked out of the camp into the streets and where usually we would have been set upon, the people simply smiled at us with our Western faces. Indeed the war was finally over, after three and a half years in the camp we were walking freely.

In order to find out what was happening across the world we went to a couple of radio shops and picked up some radios. The Radio Officers were then able to use the radios to make a decent long range set, formerly forbidden in Japan, which could be beamed across to the Philippines. Now we knew for sure that the war was over.

About six days later, on 15 August we heard the sound of aeroplanes in the distance. We had been used to the sound of B29's but this was different, these were tiny planes. They were American not Russian as some people thought. A tiny parachute was sent down out of the plane, inside which we found a message; 'Prisoners of war.Paint PW in white on your roofs - American Navy'. On later days the planes dropped food parcels as well as other items such as shoes, shirts, hair cream, even toilet paper. we had more than enough food now. Later in the week, lights were dropped for us to shine up at them. On the radio we heard that the American fleet was coming North. And so, one morning, more American planes came and out of the planes came men and women, they were marines from Britain and America as well as doctors and nursing sisters. We had never seen women in battledress before.

We were then to begin our journey home which began at Tokyo airfield. We travelled to the Philippines, across to Canada from where we sailed to Southampton. My journey ended on Lime Street Station when I met my mother, back in my Liverpool home.

Austin Morris

THE ROLE OF MOTOR LAUNCHES IN THE BATTLE OF THE ATLANTIC

The Coastal Forces branch of the Royal navy which consisted of motor torpedo boats, motor gunboats, and motor launches are well known for their stirring exploits in the Channel, the North Sea, the Mediterranean, in Greek, Yugoslavian and Italian waters, but little is known of their sterling work in the Atlantic theatre of war.

I had joined the navy at the age of seventeen and a half in February 1943 after having been a member of the Liverpool Civil Defence Corps during the Blitz, and also later as a member of the Home Guard.

The 30th M.L. Flotilla in which I served in Coastal Forces had sailed from Britain for the Caribbean in September, 1942 in response to the U-boat activity in that area, and in particular around Trinidad, which was causing concern to the Powers that were. The eight boats comprising the flotilla were the smallest warships ever to cross the Atlantic.

It was twelve months later that I joined the M.L's in Trinidad having sailed on the Queen Elizabeth to New York and thence to Norfolk, Virginia to sail on the S S 'George Washington' with other shipmates to Trinidad. We happened to dodge the U-boats on that voyage but unfortunately after we had disembarked we heard that the 'George Washington' had been sunk with no survivors, when it was on it's return journey and out of reach of the navy patrols.

The role of M.L.'s was to patrol the Gulf of Paria just inside the Bocas del Togo and occasionally to escort vessels to other islands in the Caribbean and also to the former British Guyana.

We generally worked three days out on patrol and a couple of days at the base, except when on escort duty when you could be away for some considerable time.

The stations that were patrolled were named : Zebra, Michael, George and Easy; the best stations to patrol were Zebra and Michael, they were the nearest to land while George and Easy were much further away and therefore subject to more of the rough stuff, of course the boats took it in turn to patrol the various stations.

The weather could certainly cut up rough in the Caribbean, what with the odd hurricane and water spouts to contend with. Although the B class M.L.'s were well built to stand up to anything that was thrown at them and the crews weren't so bad either!

There were times when the Liners being escorted thought that we were U-boats trying to surface rather than M.L.'s almost submerged by the heavy seas.

Apart from the aforementioned activities, M.L.'s had various other duties to perform, such as target towing for the U. S. Battlewagon Missouri en route to the Pacific or acting as targets for the midget subs (XE3 craft) also on the way to the Pacific where V.C.'s were to be won by the then Lt. Cdr M. Fraser and Leading Seaman McGennis, on sinking a Japanese cruiser.

Norman Francis Moulsdale ex Royal Navy

ACTION STATIONS

When World War Two broke out I was serving in the destroyer HMS 'Escapade' as Chief Engine Room Artificer. At this early stage of the

War the Royal Navy was very short of vessels to escort convoys of merchant ships. While frigates and corvettes were hastily being built for this purpose, fleet destroyers were often detailed for convoy protection and it was for such a duty that we arrived in Liverpool one day in 1939.

The convoy consisted of about twelve or fifteen ships in three columns. Although comparatively small, a convoy of this size would normally have an escort of about five ships - three ahead and one on each flank - but, due to the shortage of ships, HMS 'Escapade' was the only escort vessel.

As we left Gladstone Dock we were alongside a large steamer of the Royal Mail Line, the SS 'Navasota'. We went down river and the convoy assembled just off the Bar. We sailed down the Irish Sea, through the St George Channel and headed South-West into the Atlantic. We were making for a position 17° West where it was considered that the merchant ships would be reasonably safe from attack and where they would disperse and continue their voyages independently.

During the first week of November, the weather was bad and worsening all the time, we took some comfort from the fact that a U-boat attack was unlikely to be successful in such conditions.

Three days out from Liverpool during the afternoon watch, the alarm sounded and we went to 'action stations'. A ship in the convoy had been hit by a torpedo; it was the 'Navasota'. The Captain of the 'Escapade', Commander Graham R.N., immediately gave the signal for the convoy to scatter and made a circuit of the 'Navasota' to try to detect the U-boat by 'Asdics', but we were unable to get a contact and turned to help the 'Navasota'.

The 'Navasota' had been hit amidships - probably in the bunkers as a huge crack had appeared in her side and what looked like coal was tumbling out of her. Two boats had been lowered; one of which had pulled away. The Captain of the 'Navasota' was watching the operation from the bridge and made no attempt to save himself. Before the second boat could pull away the ship broke in two; the big sea that was running just seemed to tear her apart and, as the forward part of the ship went down, it took the second boat with it. The stern of the ship now rose 80 ft into the air with some of the crew frantically jumping off.

The 'Escapade' managed to get alongside the lifeboat that had pulled away just as the stern of the ''Navasota" went under. There were about twelve or thirteen men in the boat and we had great difficulty in getting them aboard because the seas were so high. Our Captain was calling through a megaphone, 'Be as quick as you can!' Of course, we were sitting targets while we were stopped, and the Captain was anxious about his own ship. We dropped a scramble net over the side but one heavy set man of about fifty kept falling back in the boat. A seaman finally attached a rope under his arms and he was dragged aboard. I spoke to this survivor later; he was an engine room greaser who, luckily had been off watch at the time. The 'Navasota's' crew were all Liverpool men but none of the deck or engineer officers survived.

We steamed around the area for a while looking for survivors. We saw some wreckage and a few bodies that were wearing the old type of Board of Trade life-jackets. These had big pieces of cork sewn into them and it appeared that when the men jumped off the stern of the ship into the water, the cork in the jackets hit them under the chin and broke their necks! I believe that this happened on other occasions and a directive was issued to the effect that the jackets should be held down at the neck with both hands when jumping into the water!

By this time the convoy was out of sight. I think the U-boat fired several torpedoes at a number of targets, but, because of the heavy seas, most of them had not run true. We landed the survivors from the 'Navasota' at Gibraltar. I saw many other ships sink as the war continued but the fate of the 'Navasota' - being the first I had seen - and the heroic action of it's Captain, who stayed on the bridge to the last, has stayed vividly in my mind.

C H Nicholls

Celebrations after the sinking of 5 U-boats. Arthur O' Leary (whose photograph this is) is towards the back on the right clearly displaying the beer bottles label !

In Memory of Joey McTeer

I joined the 'San Fernando' on the 8th April, 1941. I was picked up on 3rd June after the ship was sunk and landed at Plymouth about four days later. I was now on survivor's leave. During this time I had a drink with one of my mates who had been on the same boat as myself; his name was Joey McTeer and he was killed, with his wife and baby four days later in an air raid.

I then joined the Navy and was soon to see action in the Atlantic. Posted to Latchworth, a shore base, I passed my exams for Engine Room Petty Officer.

Following this I joined HMS 'Tracker', which was built in America, it carried 12 Avengers and 6 Wild Cats. We then took up our duties in the North Atlantic and teamed up with Escort Group 2 under the command of Captain Walker. We had much success in all the action we saw, including sinking a couple of submarines.

We were then posted to Scapa Flow, where we started escort duty with Russian Convoys, and again we saw plenty of action. Then once again we were back on escort duty with Escort Group 2 and had lots of success in sinking five U-boats.

The port of Argencia in Newfoundland was manned by Americans and they gave us a great welcome. We were still on duty by day and carried on escort duty till the end of the war.

I would like to give credit to the Fleet Arm Air Crews who did a great job; the squadron which was with us was 816.

Arthur Charles O'Leary

Engine Room Petty officer on HMS 'Tracker'

REMEMBERING THE CHILDREN OF THE 'BENARES'

I joined the Royal Navy as a boy in 1935 and served throughout the whole war. During the dark days of 1939 - 1942 I served in several ships on the Atlantic convoys. My first ship when war broke out, was the destroyer HMS 'Broke' and we escorted convoys from Liverpool to Canada. I then joined the corvette HMS 'Gloxinia' and we were stationed in Liverpool and Northern Ireland - on Atlantic Convoy work.

On Friday, September 13th, 1940 we escorted the convoy consisting of many children being evacuated to Canada on the ship 'City of Benares'. four days later she was torpedoed. Boats were lowered by the ship; 46 people were crammed into one lifeboat, including six of the children and one woman teacher. They spent the best part of ten days in the open boat in the Atlantic in atrocious weather, until being picked up by HMS 'Anthony' - one can only imagine what that lady and those children suffered in that time. The teachers name was Mary Cornish. The night of the sinking there were about 100 children on board. We could hear them screaming in the water but we could not stop for fear of submarines attacking us. So many were lost on that convoy. Feelings in Britain were sometimes against the Royal Navy escort ships because of the great loss of children. Only seamen who were there can really understand our feelings and what we went through. Later in 1941 we served in the Mediterranean between Malta and Greece. On Christmas Eve 1941, I was sent home to join a new destroyer being built at Cammel Laird, Birkenhead.

In 1943 HMS 'Scorpion' served on a few Russian convoys and was part of the fleet that was in action on Christmas Day and Boxing Day in the North Cape when we sank the German battleship 'Scharmhorst' and her escorts. We were the only ship to pick up German survivors (30 of them), hundreds of others were lost that night.

Without food, supplies and armaments brought across the 'angry' Atlantic Ocean by the Merchant Navy and the Royal Navy, the outcome of the war would have been very different; my home town of Liverpool played such an important role.

Eric J Parry

TO HALIFAX

One of my earliest trips in 1942 was joining a crew at Lime Street and travelling by train to Glasgow. After breakfast we went by coach to Greenock and boarded a Dutch liner as passengers going to a ship somewhere abroad, destination unknown.

Setting sail on this late February day we headed for Halifax, Canada and apart from the odd scare with escorts dropping depth charges, we arrived after about twelve days.

Once ashore, we went by train through snow covered countryside and after about thirty six hours reached Montreal.

We spent a further twelve days here in an hotel and then set off by train across Canada passing through many towns and prairies then on over the

Rockies. After changing trains at New Westminster near Vancouver, we travelled through California and after five days reached San Francisco.

There we found our ship the Cunarder 'Aquitania' in port and we were the new crew replacing the existing members.

Settling in, we sailed next day with an escort of two torpedo boats for twelve hours and then alone for five days until reaching Honolulu, Hawaii.

We stayed in port about a day and picked up about fifteen hundred women and children, mainly service families from Pearl Harbour. Off again we had a quite trip back to a Californian port of San Pedro where our passengers disembarked.

Leaving port we headed due South towards the Panama Canal, through it and then North towards New York. On our trip up the East coast, our escorts were very active as submarines were shelling our convoy and an oil tanker was sunk some miles away.

Reaching New York, we spent about a week at pier 90, West 50th Street and had some leave visiting cinemas, shows and shops.

Having taken on stores and about five thousand US soldiers, we headed through the North Atlantic and apart from many depth charges, arrived unscathed.

We were now on our second week in May 1942 and after a few days leave at home, off on another trip.

W G Parry

3 STORIES FROM MY BATTLE OF THE ATLANTIC

1) THE CAPTURE OF THE CREW OF U-BOAT 517- NOVEMBER 21ST 1942

On the 18th November 1942, HMS 'Opportune' left Gibraltar for the UK. She was part of the escort for the battleship 'Duke of York' and the carrier HMS 'Victorious'. We had been in the Mediterranean supporting the landings in North Africa.

On our way home through the Bay of Biscay, aircraft from the carrier 'Victorious' sighted a U-boat astern of the force. It attacked the submarine. 'Opportune' was detached from the force to investigate the sub. We were all on full alert and eventually the sub was sighted; at first it didn't seem much bigger than a dustbin. The skipper ordered small arms to be fired over the conning tower; this had the effect of speeding up the 'abandon ship' procedure. We lowered the whaler with the intentions of boarding the sub and taking it in tow. This was not to be; the sea cocks had been opened and before anything could be done about it she slipped below. As we manoeuvred the ship to pick up survivors, to our dismay they were all there in their lifebelts singing the German National Anthem. Our skipper insisted that we delay the rescue until they had finished. The rescue went off OK and there was only one casualty amongst the Germans.

They were housed in the lower forward mess deck and a guard was stationed above the hatchway. He was sat their with his canvas holster playing with the gun when he dropped it amongst the Germans. A deathly silence was observed in the mess decks above the prisoners and then an up-stretched arm handed the gun to the sentry. (Relief and laughter; he lived it down). I also recall the Commander's Iron Cross, or some such medal, had been stolen and this caused a great storm. The 'Opportune' skipper - John Le Barber was furious; he made all sorts of threats about what a shower we were, that leave would be cancelled when we reached the UK, and the culprit was asked to leave the medal in some obvious place and all would be forgiven. I don't remember if it was ever found.

Eventually we arrived in Greenock, where the prisoners were taken off; they were later shipped to Canada where they remained until after the war. They were repatriated in 1947.

Some years ago, during some of my research on the U-boat, I obtained information from the German U-boat archives. This was a private museum collection. I managed to get details of the achievements of U 517 and also the address of the former commander. I wrote to the address I had been given, not really expecting a reply, but I did get a reply and have had several letters since then. He told me of his time in prison in Canada, and of the time when he rejoined the German Navy in the early fifties. When he retired in 1975 he had become a Vice Admiral and held the rank of C-in-C of the German Fleet.

2) THE BATTLE OF THE NORTH CAPE

During the Battle of the Atlantic, I was an able seaman serving on HMS 'Opportune' which was part of the 17th Destroyer Flotilla. On 23rd December 1943, HMS 'Opportune' was part of the naval escort for Convoy RA55A sailing from the Kola Inlet in Russia. During the forenoon watch on the 26th December, HMS 'Opportune' along with HMS 'Virago', HMS 'Musketeer' and HMS 'Matchless', was instructed to leave the convoy. At the time, we did not know why, but, just before lunchtime, we were called to 'action stations' and, leaving our lunch uneaten, joined the cruisers 'Belfast', 'Sheffield' and 'Norfolk' in engaging the German battleship 'Scharnhorst'.

Our ship was stationed ahead of the cruisers because we carried eight torpedoes. I was on duty at 'A' gun and opened fire with our puny four inch guns. We were travelling at maximum speed and using life-lines. It was quite easy to see the tracer from the bigger ships' shells as they passed overhead. After chasing the 'Scharnhorst' for most of the day, our gun crew was eventually fallen-out and the torpedo crews were given target details.

By this time, the heavier covering force had arrived and the additional strength of the battleship 'Duke of York' altered the course of the battle. Everything was in complete darkness; only the flash of guns gave away the position of the enemy. When it was our turn to attack, we went straight in and delivered a salvo of four torpedoes. We veered away and came in again to fire the other four. In all we claimed three torpedo hits.

Eventually we retired and cleared the target area and it was soon confirmed that the 'Scharnhorst' had sunk. Apart from ships already mentioned, other British forces included the cruiser 'Janace' and the destroyers 'Savage', 'Saumarez', 'Scorpion' and 'Sword'. Needless to say, when we arrived back in the mess, our uneaten lunch just floated past in pools of water - accompanied by the odd sock! After the signal to 'Splice the Mainbrace' had been given we steamed into Scapa Flow where the home fleet cheered us all to our respective berths. The sinking of the 'Scharnhorst' removed one of the greatest threats to the Northern Allied convoys and enabled the redeployment of ships that had always to be at hand because of the constant menace of that great German battleship.

3) CONVOY RA53 - NORTH RUSSIA to LOCH EWE

Left Kola Inlet - 1st March, 1943 - Arrived UK 14th March, 1943

Consisting of some 30 merchant ships, we left the Kola Inlet on 1st March, 1943. It was known that U-boats were in the area and after a few days out, we lost the merchant ship 'Executive', the 'Richard Bland' was also damaged.

The convoy suffered many attacks by Junkers 88's but was supported by a strong escort which put up a strong barrage of fire which persuaded the enemy to retire. There were reports of several U-boats being in the area, the merchant ship 'Puerto Regan' was torpedoed. It was also stated at the time that the 'Richard Bland' had sunk. The weather deteriorated and several ships suffered storm damage.

As we were nearing Iceland and close to our own minefields, the merchant ship, SS 'John H B Latrobe', which was one of the ships to suffer storm damage, was drifting helplessly into the minefield, our ship, HMS 'Opportune', Commander John Le Barber, was instructed to go to the assistance of the merchant ship.

This operation required a delicate manoeuvre and involved seamanship at it's best. Our skipper, John Le Barber, directed the operations and in very bad weather and trying conditions, we approached the stricken vessel. Heavy towing tackle was prepared and eventually we managed to secure a tow line. In the meantime, several of the crew of HMS 'Opportune' were lying flat out on the fo'c'sle peering over the side to warn of any mines that were evident; this was a very precarious job but it was realised later that it was an essential duty.

It was at this time that all eyes were on the towing gear as the heavy ropes began to take the strain, and, safely and surely, we crept out of the minefield to safety, the relief on our faces must have been apparent. It was possibly after a day and a half that we reached the relative safety of Seidisfiord, Iceland.

Later on we were to hear that our skipper, John Le Barber had received special commendation from the Commander in Chief, Home Fleet, Admiral Tovy.

As an Able Seaman, I received the princely sum of £1.8s for rendering assistance.

William Leonard Phillips

THROWN IN AT THE DEEP END

I joined the Merchant Service at seventeen years of age in late 1943. I first enrolled as a trainee at the Sea Training School at Withens Lane, Wallasey, in company with many young lads like myself. They must have been desperate for men, as in less than a month we were considered full trained and fit to go to sea as junior ordinary seamen.

We accordingly joined the seamen's pool at Cornhill in Liverpool where no time was wasted in sending us to Greenock, Scotland, for a brief gunnery course of two days before we joined our ships.

My first voyage was on what was termed awn iron-ore carrier, to North Africa via the Bay of Biscay for a full cargo of iron ore. One old A/B informed me that this was not a very popular cargo with seamen, as iron-ore carriers sank very quickly indeed when torpedoed. Thankfully, we reached home safely this time.

From that time on I made many voyages from the Home Country across the Atlantic to America and Canada. At one time I was a crew member on a merchant aircraft carrier escorting convoys to and from Halifax, Nova Scotia. There were a small number of these ships, which were merchant ships which had had their superstructures removed and a flight deck added. In addition to their escort duties, they also carried a cargo of grain. They carried four or five Swordfish aircraft which were there to patrol the convoy as an anti-submarine measure. The carrier I served on was the 'Empire McDermott', whose flight deck was approximately four hundred and fifty feet long, making take off and landing no mean feat.

In fact, my admiration for the very young pilots was unbounded, as to land an aircraft on the rolling, pitching, short flight deck seemed to me a miracle at times. I still remember them with pride and admiration. I saw the war out with service in many theatres of war before the end of hostilities, and was en-route from Burma to what was then French Indo-China when the war in Europe ended.

L Redfern

SOUTHAMPTON - LIVERPOOL - FREETOWN - PORT SAID

We arrived at Lime Street Station in the early hours of the morning, cold, hungry and tired; more like refugees than soldiers. We had been bombed out of Southampton.

The port had been our headquarters, our billets, a school. We were No. 3 Company Trooping Pool, R.A.M.C. ex St John Ambulance trained, and then one month Aldershot Parade Ground trained. I have a copy of the War Office Directive stating that we were specially selected by the War Office. Perhaps they were right, but at that moment we had our own feelings, with Liverpool and Glasgow the only two ports left open, and on our own. So, with our thoughts, we marched off to be stationed at a Disabled Home in Parliament Street, next to the Rialto Cinema, which we all thought a good omen. The Headquarters Staff took over the Home while the rest of us were billeted in Percy Street with the Sergeants Mess in Huskisson Street.

Sefton Park was used as a parade ground, the Rialto for tea dances and dances held by the Pioneers at barracks in Dingle Lane School. On 2/- a day we had it made! Then the Western Approaches Command was set up, and so we, in our small way, were in business. We trained for our certificates for 3rd Class and 2nd Class and went to sea. The size of the ship or liner determined the amount of troops it carried, and also the number of medical staff. Some of the guns were manned by ship's stewards.

The ship carried what was called a submarine gun, but it was understood by all, and by the D.E.M.S. gunner that if they fired the gun, they would be tipped over the side. The gun - pre-1914, stood aft, over the Isolation Ward, and when fired during practice, the Ward shook and the patients took a very dim view of being deafened and shaken out of bed, but it did keep the bed count down. Troops arrived at the Liverpool Landing Stage by train; a ring of M.P.'s surrounded everybody as security was paramount. They left the train carrying kit and rifle which were later handed in at the armoury. One incident still remains in my mind; a soldier handing a letter to a docker whilst in the process of going on board. Everything stopped, D.E.M.S., medical staff and a percentage of troops going aboard were ordered to parade at the double on the Landing Stage for what I was informed afterwards, was a 'Drum Head' court-martial with drum. Very impressive, but a stupid thing to do, but in those days things were happening so fast, you were being told to do this and ordered to do that without explanation.

Because the odds were against us, we were all inwardly very scared. We were all accustomed now to being bombed on land, but at sea, and also with submarines as well, the odds were stacked too high; besides who ever heard of a soldier cum sailor?

As soon as we loaded up we stood in the River Mersey, the main reason being to stop the troops escaping; and many tried. The ship was called the 'Duchess of York'. It was the first time I had witnessed such opulence. The panelling, pictures, the gilded staircase, were wonders to behold; a cockney kid in such surroundings! Cabins had been ripped out to make approximately twenty or more beds for our main ward and the M.I. Room. The O.R.'s slept below us.

Life on board ship needed a sense of humour & Captain's rounds started the day, below decks and hospital included. The ship carried a full compliment of army personnel, C. O. Major, RSM and orderly Room Staff. Guards were stationed at all gangways for blackout and security regulations, and also a good part of the ship was out of bounds.

Medical Staff consisted of S.M.O., M.O., S.M., Sgt. Clerk, Sgt. Dispenser, Corporal Six Nursing Orderlies; the O.R.'s were only allowed in the hospital area and on the main deck, not the sun deck. Getting a hair cut was a money making business, a pair of clippers, scissors, a box and a mate, and you were made. If you did not know how to cut hair, you soon learnt on our customers, and they were unable to escape, first it was 3d at time and then 6d.

Everybody had a racket. It took a few weeks for everybody to settle down to a routine, that the ships orderly room had written out in daily orders. It took nearly a month to reach our first port of call which was Freetown. Water barges came out and water was taken on board. You filled your water bottle up at the times stated, if you didn't, you relied on your mate.

Troop convoys were understood to be fast convoys, but in the convoy, ships carried the equipment of the troops, and the command could only use the ships that they had at the time. Hence, you always had a number of coal burning ships which gave out plenty of smoke, and the Commodore's ship's siren kept squawking by the hour telling you to stop.

Having left Freetown, we made a detour to avoid the sub-pens in the French Atlantic Ports (we hoped), to our next port which was to be Capetown for one half, and Port Elizabeth for the other half of the Convoy. Capetown, and what a reception the people gave to the troops, everybody had shore leave, and when we sailed away, who could not forget the good kindly lady who sang the ships out of the harbour from the end of the pier. She remains in the memory of every soldier

At night the heat was building up between decks, and the O.R.'s slept where they could to escape it, in the gangways, even on deck, the heat became oppressive.

But at first light, those who slept on deck, had to roll up their bedding as the seaman started to hose down the decks. Orders came over the ships tannoy about sunbathing, and anybody getting sunburnt would have his name and number taken when he reports for treatment, and so out came the Calamine Oil and brush, Gentient Violet for Doby itch.

Regarding feeding on board ship, dinnertime consisted mostly of stew plus one baked potato. Why was the Lancashire soil left on the potatoes? Was it to remind us of England and what we were fighting for; and the bread, never cut the bread, always break it, that way you never cut a cockroach in half.

On to Port Said, we had made it, the troops went ashore and we sailed for home We never learn, as we left Capetown, a few days out, stories circulated on board ship, that sinking had taken place of ships that had left earlier from the same convoy. So the ship headed for the nearest port of call which was Pernambuco, South America. From there in convoy we sailed for home, and as we entered the Mersey, with the first sighting of the Liver Birds, everything was O.K.

Back to Parliament Street to be told to report to Gladstone Dock and the Winchester Castle - a new ship, a new company.

The ships I sailed in were 'Arundel Castle', 'Brittanic', 'Scythia', 'Orian', 'Emberence Bay', 'Takliwa', 'Felix Roussel', 'Duchess of York', 'Winchester Castle'.

Mr H W Richards, ex Cpl RAMC
No: 3 Company Trooping Pool 7567915

MV 'WILLIAM WILBERFORCE' (ELDER DEMPSTER)

Engagement 17.9.1942 Discharge 9.1.1943 (At sea)

I joined the ship at Liverpool signing on as a Deck Boy. We left the 'Pool' and joined a convoy travelling to Freetown in Africa. There we spent a month or so sailing up and down the West coast dropping off cargo and picking up ground nuts, palm oil and teak for home. When fully laden, we headed back home from Lagos.

Three or four days out of Lagos, a column of smoke was spotted. It appeared that a ship must have been on fire, so a lookout was kept for any signs of wreckage. None was found.

One day, after tea time, I went amidships to borrow a book from the cook who was preparing dinner for the saloon. He told me that I would find the book in his cabin, so I headed off to the cabin where I found the book. However, just as I picked the book up there was a tremendous explosion, followed closely by a second. The ship shuddered and lights went out. I stumbled into the alley having dropped the book and ran towards the galley. The ship listed to starboard as I ran through the galley causing me to fall headlong onto the floor which was now covered with food. I quickly picked myself up and headed for the boat deck.

I arrived at the boat deck as the A.B's were lowering the boats on the port side. I managed to jump into one. However, the boat I was in started to take in water. Evidently the heat had dried the planks out so much that the lifeboats had little gaps where the water had bubbled through so we bailed the water out. As this was happening the back of the ship was hastily disappearing under the water, dragging the remainder of the ship with it.

Someone noticed a large black shape lying on the water behind us and shouted for our attention. We turned and looked, but it was difficult to tell what it was in the darkness. Until that is, someone shone a light across the water. It lit up other lifeboats, but we were unprepared for what we saw. There, not more than 400 foot away was the submarine that had sunk our ship. From the conning tower of the submarine a figure called out a series of questions. He wanted to know the name of the ship, her cargo, where we were heading and also whether there were any officers in the boats. We told him that most of the officers had in fact gone down with the ship. Most of the crew shouted back 'peanuts' and various obsceni- ties. He remarked that he did not understand and pointed what looked like a Lewis gun (attached to the conning tower) at us. This almost casual threat lead to him getting the answers he required. When he had got the information he required, he disappeared and not long after so did the submarine.

All night we continued to bail the water out of our boat before it finally sealed up. When morning arrived, we roped together our boat to a motor launch, packed with other survivors. We proceeded to power our way in the direction of land. Sadly though, we ran out of petrol. A decision was made that it would be best to separate once more. Passengers from the ship that had taken refuge in our boat were put in the other with the Captain, and some of the crew were transferred to ours. We rowed away taking turns at the oars. Fortunately, we had some rations of water, Ovaltine tablets, and some small biscuits. These were shared out amongst us.

As the days passed, some of the African crew appeared to be suffering more than us, as one or two of them had taken to drinking the salt water. The days passed without further incident. The days being really hot, contrasting dramatically with the cold nights. Each day we rowed and drifted and still no ships appeared to help us.

It was on the seventh day that we were espied by a Spanish ship. We were taken aboard and questioned about further survivors. We told them about the other boat and so set off in search of them. After five more hours, we managed to find the motor boat.

The Spanish ship took us the Canary Islands and we remained there for a few weeks until we managed to get a Spanish passenger ship to Gibraltar. From there, the troop ship 'Letita' brought us home to England.

There were 61 crew in the two boats, also four women and two male passengers who were missionaries. We lost only one man during this incident... the purser during the night of torpedoing. He was a kind man, always having time for a word and a joke, and I have never forgotten him.

Mr G S Roberts

THE 'ALDEN GIFFORD'

Engagement 30.6.1944 Discharge 20.9.1944 (Ship Wreck)

Joined the ship at Liverpool to voyage around the coast of Britain, stopping and visiting ports at Cardiff, Bristol, Birkenhead, Barry and Devonport.

During our voyages, a number of faults with regard to winches not holding, and Blokes jamming occurred. It led me to thinking that the ship required docking and a comprehensive overhaul. However, it was after our last port of call, Barry, where we had picked up a load of coal destined for Devonport, that the 'Alden Gifford' was to begin its final journey.

We departed from Barry in very rough weather. The wind was strong and getting stronger. I happened to be on the 4pm to 8pm watch when the gale force winds loosened the hatch covers and the tarpaulin started to blow off. The crew were all turned out to make them fast. Ropes were placed across the canvas over the hatch boards to hold them down, which seemed to do the trick.

My watch finished without further incident and my mate Jock and I returned to our cabin to change into dry clothes. Just as we were climbing into our bunks a large wave came over the side of the ship onto the deck. The water rushed down the stairs washing us out of our cabin. As the water dissipated, we grabbed as much dry gear as we could and moved into the warmth and dryness of the messroom but the next minutes we heard a voice shouting; 'She's going!' The voice belonged to the cook, a friend of Jocks.

Jock and I both rushed up onto the deck as were on the falls on (ie: responsible for) the lifeboat on the starboard side.

On the way to the boat deck we tried in vain to release a raft. Although the lever moved, the raft remained where it was, so we carried on to the boat station. Arriving at the boat station, we noticed the boats were still in. No one had swung them out. The men that were there explained through the wind that they had tried to remove the davits but could not move them. Suddenly the ship rolled onto the port side. I slid down the deck to the other side. The lifeboat was there, under water, I balanced myself on a davit post which was across the lifeboat and decided to dive into the tempestuous sea.

There were hatch boards floating about so I swam and grabbed one using it like a surfboard I paddled until I was safely away from the ship.

The ship went down very quickly, though a raft rose to the surface. I abandoned the hatch cover and swam to the life raft which I climbed into.

Whilst huddling on the raft, I noticed a chap swimming towards the raft. He made it, and I pulled him in. We sat huddled together till a French fisherman returning from a nights fishing cam by. He circled around us a few times and shouted through a hailer to jump and catch his boat, which we did and his crew pulled us aboard.

The seamanship of that little boat was marvellous as he went around picking up further survivors from wreckage and hatch boards. Evidently he had seen the ship going down and had radioed ashore for a lifeboat. The lifeboat arrived not long after and took some men off him as we sailed into Penzance.

There we received a pleasant cup of tea from the WVS who were on the quay. Only dressed in a vest and dungarees, I was taken with others to the nearest hospital.

As far as I am aware, the Frenchman had come over to Penzance on his fishing vessel during the war to make a home in Penzance. I wonder if he succeeded?

Mr G S Roberts

HMS BULOLO

During the Second World War I was in the RAF and served aboard HMS 'Bulolo' which had a ships company of army, navy and RAF.

HMS 'Bulolo' was a combined operations headquarters ship designed for amphibious landings on enemy coasts. We sailed the Atlantic many times, to and from operations in the Mediterranean area, usually in large convoys. The convoys consisted of merchant ships carrying troops and equipment with naval escorts of sloops, destroyers, cruisers, aircraft carriers and battleships.

On many occasions, evasive action had to be taken due to the presence of U-boats. My own ship carried depth charges which were rolled off the stern and these lifted that part of the ship out of the water by the force of the explosion.

We often encountered bad weather and ships on the horizon would disappear from view in the huge swells. It was amazing how the aircraft carriers managed to launch their planes in such conditions. Feeding the crew also caused problems in very rough weather. They frequently lost all their food from the mess tables as the ship pitched and rolled.

N. Roberts

ONE OF MANY

My memory of the Battle of the Atlantic took place when I was on the troopship 'Leopoldville' taking me to West Africa to join an RAF Squadron of Coastal Command Sunderland Flying Boats.

For five days in December, we endured dreadful weather conditions, battling against the elements of the notorious Bay of Biscay. Even the crew said that it was exceptionally bad, and what all these men went through I will never forget for the rest of my life.

It was 23 December 1943 when I, and many more of my friends had the privilege to go to an ENSA party, who were travelling abroad to entertain the troops in different parts of the world. They did a good job and they invited us to a show in the canteen. We were just beginning to enjoy the show and having a good laugh with some of the lads trying to take part in the show, (there were a number of women in the show, I thought they were tough, doing this job living in these terrible conditions). Suddenly, the whole ship shook. We could hear the ships metal plates banging with the report. The girls on stage screamed. It startled them and they went pale and I admit it shook us all up. I started to get some funny ideas into my head. Is this it? Is this here and now the end of the journey? Then we heard the sound of the alarm. 'All muster to boat stations, submarine warning'. As soon as everybody heard this they didn't know what to do. All the previous practice runs had been forgotten. I thought there was going to be a panic; the women started shouting, one cool person said 'Keep calm!' as a number of men tried to rush the stairs to take them on top. 'Keep calm' was the order. So we got our senses together and in an orderly manner we proceeded to the boat stations, calmly and in record time. Everybody was shaky because at this time the situation could have been a lot worse. If the ship had been hit I don't think many would have got out. I saw panic there for the first time, and it was a cool head that saved the situation.

Depth charges had been dropped and a submarine was in the vicinity, a bit too close. Again we heard the reports and the ship's plates shuddered and left a ringing in our ears. I think at this moment, my life passed before me. Standing on deck, not knowing what might happen to us all at any minute, I looked at the rafts which we were allotted to, stared at them hard, and realised that if anything did happen, these rafts were not enough, or big enough to take the personnel. Maybe some would survive, but the majority would perish in the elements of the sea; sharks and cold water. After about one and a half hours waiting at the boat stations, we were put at ease when the 'All Clear' was sounded and were told to dismiss. Afterwards we heard that our escort had either destroyed the submarine or they had given it a rough time. Once more we were in debt to the navy.

It is now 46 years since my story took place, and in that time I have asked myself many questions as regards what did really take place and happen to the Leopoldville Convoy OS62-KMS 36. What did really happen on the day in December 1943 that we had the boat station alarm which caused such a panic at the time? How near were we to destruction? and what part did the navy really play in our protection for our safety?

Through many channels, and with the help of the naval and maritime records, and various books in the library, I was able to build up a picture as to what really did happen to the convoy to West Africa which for so many years I could not answer.

I know how many brave men gave their lives for their fellow men. Lives were lost in the protection of this convoy and many U-boats and enemy aircraft were involved. This, in December 1943, when standing at boat stations, I did not know. Again, we thanked the Navy and also the US Navy for our protection at a very serious time, but these brave men would only say that they were doing their job as one of many.

It is recorded that the Convoy OS62-KMS 36 was, on December 22 1943 right across the paths of the Borkum Group of U-boats, consisting of thirteen submarines which were also patrolling and looking to give protection to a blockage runner heading for Bordeaux with a load of tin and rubber vital to the German war machine. These U-boats were there to escort the blockage runners but had come right across the path of the African convoy. Also in the vicinity, was the American aircraft carrier 'Card' with her screen escorts. The German U-boat Commander - Doenitz then decided the aircraft carrier was more important so the U-boats attacked the carrier, Borkum Group consisted of U107, U618, U270, U541, U645, U962, U415, U275, U382, U641, U305, U801, U667.

The weather at the time was hurricane gales which did not allow aircraft to be launched. These gales continued for a number of days and the convoy, for its protection, had to be diverted off its course on account of the U-boats and enemy aircraft from German land bases, which were in the vicinity.

One of the screens to the aircraft carrier 'Card', the USS 'Leary', made contact with the U-boats but they attacked with torpedoes, missed the ACC 'Card' and hit the USS 'Leary', which was sunk by the U-boat 275. Also HMS ' Hurricane' made contact with two U-boats and went to engage them, HMS 'Hurricane' being the senior destroyer in the group. It was known that she attacked at full speed which was at the time, a mistake, and the U-boat 415 fired a torpedo which homed onto her rudder, making her powerless and sinking her. Thank God, survivors were taken to other ships; but the 'Leary' was not so fortunate. She was hit in the engine room and the hold. Then came along U-boat 382 which fired another torpedo and destroyed her completely.

Many years later, I was to learn that the ship, the 'Leopoldville', that we went to Africa on, was sunk, something I was shocked and sorry to hear about, but again in war. These men were only some of many who had given their lives. Me and all of my friends spent Christmas on the 'Leopoldville' at Gibraltar in 1943. One year later on Christmas Eve 1944 she was torpedoed and sunk by U486, five and a half miles off Cherbourg, while carrying 2235 US troops and escorted by HMS 'Brilliant' and 'Anthony'. The former took off a number of troops before the vessel sank but of the troops, 802 were lost and, of her crew of 237, 17 - including the master were killed. What a tragedy. The U-boat 486, which sank the troopship 'Leopoldville' with the devastating loss of life was also presumed lost herself by submarine attack of the coast of Norway in April 1945 with the loss of all hands.

J Thompson

BEFORE CONVOYS: SHIP SUNK BY ENEMY ACTION: SS 'STATESMAN - 17TH MAY 1941

My memory is of my small part in the Merchant Navy, before they had convoys, when we sailed on our own.

Waking early one morning, we were attacked by a German plane; bombed, torpedoed, machine gunned and then sunk. We did get two of the lifeboats away and I forget how many hours we were in the water. We were picked up by the SS 'Trojan Star' and then transferred to a navy corvette and taken to Londonderry, Ireland. We stayed there one night and then back to Liverpool. After a short leave home, back to sea. Next stop - North Africa.

Steward F F Walker

THE GREATEST GERMAN THAT EVER LIVED

In 1941 aged 16, I made my first trip to sea as a cabin boy on the MV 'Port Montreal'. We did three round trips to Canada, Australia and New Zealand. We carried various cargoes from each country. On our third trip, outward bound from Canada to Australia, our ship was torpedoed. It was 10th June, 1942 and just breaking into daylight when it happened. After swimming amongst the wreckage I found a life raft and then I was picked up by a lifeboat and all seemed safe and well until, to our dismay, we heard a thundering sound and saw the bows of a U-boat surface not far away from the lifeboat. We were all thrown into a state of panic having heard tales of lifeboats being machine gunned or rammed by U-boats. The Commander of the U-boat hailed us and asked us the name of our ship, port of registration, tonnage, cargo and destination. Then he simply bade us farewell and safe landing; all eyes were transfixed as the U-boat went back into the waves. To us men on the lifeboat, that Commander was the greatest German that ever lived as he spared us our lives.

In the days that followed, some men perished in those overcrowded lifeboats (we had previously used some lifeboats in the rescue of survivors from an American ship, so the lifeboats were very overcrowded). We had to give those that perished a watery grave and all the men would watch as the body floated away. We were eventually picked up and landed in Panama from whence we were shipped to New York and we all went our different ways to sail the seven seas once again.

J Wall

MEMORIES OF THE NORTH AND SOUTH ATLANTIC

At nineteen years of age I was in my fifth week of training for the Royal Artillery at Towyn, North Wales, when everyone was taken to the local cinema to see a film of convoys at sea. After the film, volunteers to become gunners on ships were called for - Bill Kelly from Birkenhead; Joe Noden from West Derby; myself, and a chap whose name I don't remember were the only ones to stand up.

After anti-aircraft gun training in North Shields, Billy Kelly and I were sent to Warwick Street, Liverpool to await a posting. We joined a Dutch ship called 'Ganemeadus', whose guns were mounted on top of a thirty foot cylinder on the boat deck. We certainly had a bird's eye view!

As we sailed out of Liverpool, my mind went back to the rowing boats on the park lakes. 'What a contrast to this!", I thought. Little did I know what was to come. So far, we had only encountered small waves and rolls as we reached the Bar Lightship. Out in the Atlantic it was a different story and, carrying only ballast, the ship rose and fell alarmingly. One minute I would be looking down on the other ships in the convoy looking just like rowing boats on a lake, the next I would be in a deep trough with water all around me. I will never forget that until the day die!

About nine days out of Liverpool, the Chief Engineer went down with acute appendicitis, which meant that our ship and one of the destroyer escorts dropped out of the convoy so that he could be transferred to the latter. The destroyer then left us and we made full speed to rejoin the convoy. It was a weird experience being all alone out there in the middle of the Ocean. We were bound for Halifax, Nova Scotia and then Boston, Massachusetts - a journey of some 3,500 miles.

On arrival at Boston, we were greeted very warmly as we tied up. Almost immediately the dockers came aboard and started loading the cargo. Quite soon the holds and decks were full of trucks of all shapes and sizes. Wooden catwalks were erected over the deck cargo for easier movement around the ship and then off we were back to Blighty again - with that feeling in the pit of your stomach as you would wonder if you would ever sea home again.

My next trip was to Algeria and our convoy lost one ship in the Bay of Biscay and another in the Mediterranean. After that, I volunteered for service in the Far East and was there for nearly three years before I eventually sailed home again via South America.

Tom Williams

RECOLLECTIONS OF COASTAL COMMAND, R.A.F.

From mid-June to mid-November, 1943 I served as a navigator with No. 269 Squadron R.A.F. at Reykjavik, Iceland. The squadron had moved to Iceland in 1941 and was equipped with the Lockheed Hudson. Previously basedate Kaldadarnes on the South Coast of Iceland, flooding in Spring 1943 forced a move to Reykjavik. Before moving to Iceland, the squadron operated from Wick, Northern Scotland.

The Hudson was an American two-engined aircraft derived from a successful airliner, the Lockheed 14 Electra. Because of this, it was considerably roomier than most of the military aircraft of World War Two and, though equipped to R.A.F. standards, which were generally spartan so far as crew comfort was concerned, the Hudson was relatively comfortable for the crew. For the navigator it had the great advantage that from his normal station in the nose he had a wide angled view in all directions.

No. 269 Squadron had already earned the distinction of several U-boat kills and the capture of U-570 (later used by the Royal Navy as HMS Graph) when I joined in June 1943.

Prior to my posting to Iceland I had served as a navigator on the Hampden torpedo bomber at Leuchars on the East coast of Scotland. The task there was to attack shipping and to act as strike force to prevent German naval units from breaking out into the Atlantic. The squadron did carry out other operational duties and in May 1943 a Hampden of 455 Squadron sank a U-boat off the Faeroe Islands.

I had transferred to the RAF in April 1941 for aircrew training, after serving in the T.A. from August 1939, and eventually went to Canada for navigation training. This included recognition, and ended at 32 Operation Training Unit, R.A.F. at Patricia Bay, Vancouver Island. At the O.T.U. crews were formed, and, apart from further navigational exercises, there was practice in torpedo dropping. Our final night navigation exercise in July 1942 resulted in air raid warnings being sounded in the U.S.A.'s Western coastal state of Washington as low cloud prevented recognition of our intended landfall and all aircraft on the exercise appeared to be approaching the sensitive Seattle-Tacoma area.

Return to the U.K. was made in the Queen Mary from New York to the Clyde and was followed by a further spell of torpedo training before joining No. 144 Squadron at Leuchars. No. 144 were taken off operational duties soon after I joined them and the pilots were posted to a conversion unit to learn to fly the Bristol Beaufighter. I remained at Leuchars to fly with 455 Squadron and was eventually posted to Reykjavik where I joined a crew on arrival with a captain, like myself from Merseyside, who had already flown as second pilot on 120 Squadron equipped with the four-engine Liberator. Despite frequent bad weather, flying was very intensive. The main task at that time was to fly standing patrols between Iceland and the Faeroes to force U-boats on passage to and from their bases to remain submerged for long periods and thus slow down there movement. By the middle of 1943, some of the weaknesses of the anti-submarine operations by aircraft had been solved; the depth charge was now an effective weapon and the Hudson was gradually being equipped with the rocket projectile (R.P.). To aid detection of U-boats, the Hudson used A.S.V. (Air to Surface vessel) Radar, though U-boats now had search receivers which could detect radar transmissions. Radar was also a great aid to the navigator when returning to base as the ninety nautical mile range enabled the accuracy of the landfall to be checked. Improvements in armaments and search methods led to greater numbers of sightings, attacks and sinkings, resulting in a reduction in U-boat attacks on ships.

During my time in Iceland, I flew on almost forty operational sorties but never saw a U-boat! The only occasion which could have been a sighting, in July 1943, was an unexpected encounter with the forces of nature. On a stormy day, when the swells were running high, and the blown spray was limiting visibility so that our visual search was handicapped, we sighted a disturbance on the surface which called for rapid investigation - it could have been the swirl left by a crash-diving U-boat. Diving down to attack height of fifty feet, the Hudson suddenly was seized by some invisible force which flung it skywards at tremendous speed, only to fall as rapidly almost immediately. Luckily the fall checked before the plane reached sea level, the engines seemed unharmed and everything else was functioning normally, so we quickly reported to base and asked for medical aid on our return. Despite much speculation as to the cause of this strange incident, no clear conclusion was reached, but the crew's opinion was that we had tangled with an embryo waterspout.

As a precaution against 'ditching' before a position signal could be sent, two homing pigeons in special containers were carried on every sortie. Each bird had a small message capsule attached to one leg. Messages flown back to the home loft in several cases resulted in the downed crew being rescued. While working on the Blue Funnel berth at South Gladstone Dock some years after the war, one of the quay foremen turned out to have been the pigeon keeper at Reykjavik loft!

No: 269 Squadron claims the distinction of being the most successful anti-submarine squadron operating Hudson aircraft. Apart from U570, the Squadron is credited with four definite 'kills' and three damaged U-boats. In the earlier period of the war, the Squadron claimed four successes but there is some doubt about these. However, it is likely that two of these are U122 and U102, which are recorded as being lost by unknown causes at the relevant dates of the attacks by '269' aircraft.

David Withey

Chapter 2
The Battle at Sea
Friends and relatives remember

MY FATHER - Carpenter on SS "Andania"

My father, David Houston was the carpenter on the SS 'Andania'; an armed merchant cruiser escorting convoys across the North Atlantic. Unfortunately, the vessel was torpedoed and wrecked on 16 June, 1940.

My father went down to the engine room to check no one had been left behind, slipped on a wet ladder rung and broke his ankle, although it was a fortnight later before he would admit that it felt like more than a sprain!

An Icelandic fishing vessel picked up the crew. There was a heart stopping moment when the German submarine surfaced; luckily it did not do any more damage. The crew were given corned beef to eat, but the men were packed together so tightly in the cramped conditions that it was difficult for them to raise their arms and almost impossible to eat.

Thankfully no lives were lost.

My father was awarded the BEM and died in 1968 aged 77 years.

May Affleck

Photographs from convoy PQ17 (Top) on D-Day. The reverse of the photos taken by the ships official photographer contained the following warning "R.N. offficial photograph , crown Copyright reserved. Not to be communicated to the press.

CAPTAIN WILLIAM PAUL BOYLAN

My late father, Captain William Paul Boylan commanded the steamer 'Yorktown' on convoy RB41 (also known as convoy 'Maniac' - you had to be mad etc...) which sailed from Halifax, Nova Scotia in September, 1942 bound for the Clyde. The following is his report on what happened on that journey.

S. J. Boylan

SHIPPING CASUALTIES SECTION - TRADE DIVISION
REPORT OF AN INTERVIEW WITH THE MASTER,
CAPTAIN W. P. BOYLAN

SS 'YORKTOWN' — 1,547 Gross Tons
CONVOY RB1 — Sunk by torpedo from U-boat on 26th September, 1942

CAPTAIN W P BOYLAN

We were bound from St. Johns, Newfoundland, to Londonderry in ballast. We were armed with 1 - 12pdr., 4 Oerlikons and 4 PAC Rockets. The Confidential Books were in a weighted bag and went down with the ship. The number of crew, including 5 Naval and 5 Military Gunners was 62, of whom the 2nd Engineer was injured and 18 are missing, including the 2nd officer, 4th engineer, Chief W/T officer, 1 Naval and 1 Military Gunner.

We left St Johns on 21 September at 14.00 sailing in a special convoy RB1. There were 8 ships in this convoy which was sailing in 4 columns and our position was no; 31.

Nothing of incident occurred until the afternoon of 24th September when the Commodore made a signal that we were being shadowed by a submarine and that we could expect an attack during the night. No attack developed and we proceeded without incident until about 1400 on 25 September when the Commodore's ship the 'Boston' was struck by 2 torpedoes on the port side, blew up and sank in about 7 minutes. While this ship was sinking, the tracks of 2 torpedoes were seen, one passed ahead of us and the other one astern. I immediately put the helm hard over to starboard, and one torpedo passed about 30ft ahead of my ship and one about 15 foot from the stern. The 'President Warfield' no; 41 in the convoy was firing at the torpedoes with her 12 pdr, and machine guns.

After this attack, the convoy scattered and the 2 destroyer escorts circled and commenced dropping depth charges. About 1600 on the same day the convoy was reformed and the Vice Commodore in the 'New York' took charge. We reformed into 4 columns and I took up position as the leading ship of the outside port column.

We proceeded without further incident until 2000 on 25 September when the chains of my steering gear became fouled on the drum of the steering engine and we were forced to stop. The engineers went below to effect repairs when about 2100 two violent explosions seemed to take place on our starboard side which were both felt and heard. The explosions were almost simultaneous and I think they took place very close to the ship and were probably caused by two torpedoes exploding at the end of their run. I immediately went on deck and could see snow flakes and gun flashes from the convoy which was now about 12 miles away.

By 2200 the steering gear was repaired and I decided not to keep to the convoy track, but steered North for about 30 miles and at 2330 25th September, I altered course to pick up the stragglers' route.

Everything went well until 22 GMT (2050 Convoy time) on the 26 September when in position 55° 10'N. - 18° 50'W. we were struck by a torpedo on the port side immediately underneath the bridge. The sea at the time was very rough with a high swell and wind WNW force 6, the sky was overcast and visibility was about 2 miles. The degaussing was on at the time and we were proceeding at twelve and a half knots on a course 081° (true).

I was in my room lying down and everything collapsed around me, I had great difficulty in struggling out through the mass of debris. When I got on deck, I found that all the superstructure forward of the bridge, which was made of wood, had collapsed, including the bridge. The engines had stopped immediately and very soon after I reached the deck the ship began to crack and rend which I thought was no; 2 bulkhead giving way. The ship sank within about 3 minutes.

The starboard' midships boat was lowered but for some unknown reason it promptly capsized; fortunately there was nobody in it. We tried to get No; 1 boat away but the davits were twisted and it was impossible to do so.

The ship sank so rapidly that there was no time to get to any of the boats and I had to jump into the water and was swimming about for an hour until I saw a raft and swam towards it. The Chief Engineer and Fireman were on this raft and they quickly pulled me on to it. From this raft we could see many red lights in the water, so we commenced to paddle around and by 1500 had taken 19 men on to our raft. The last man to be picked up was the 2nd Wireless Operator and by this time the raft was so crowded that this man said be preferred to stay where he was hanging on to a piece of wooden deck house which had floated off the ship.. Very few of the crew were wearing their lifebelts as the ship had sunk very quickly before they had time to collect them.

When daylight came, I could see three other rafts floating about. The Mate and 3rd mate who were on one of these rafts with about 12 men pulled over to us. We saw another raft with only 3 men on it, so the Mate said he would paddle over and bring it over to us, after which we could even out the numbers on each raft. The Mate managed to get to this other raft, but owing to the heavy seas he was unable to tow it back again. I think there were also 2 men on a fourth raft, but they were too far away to be able to get to them.

Some of the crew who were still left in the water got hold of a water logged boat, righted it and managed to bale it out dry. Eleven men got into this boat and they picked up the two men from the fourth raft and took the provisions from the raft.

At noon on 27th September we were still crowded on our raft when a large-engineered bomber flew over us; it looked like a 'Flying Fortress.' It came down and circled round us and a ‘Mae West’ with provision was dropped to each raft, but we were unable to paddle to the one nearest us.

We remained on the rafts for the rest of that day and at daylight on 28 September we found that a fireman had died during the night.

About 1900 on 28 September the destroyer ‘Sardonix’ arrived and picked us up after we had been on the raft for 48 hours. When we got on board this destroyer, everything possible was done for us, and nothing was too much trouble. We proceeded on board HMS ‘Sardonix’ and landed at Londonderry on 29 September.

We had water and biscuits on the rafts and also some chocolate and a small tin of Horlicks malted milk tablets. I gave the men 1 dipper of water three times a day and our evening meal consisted of chocolate, Horlicks malted milk tablets and biscuits.

We had no means of attracting attention on the raft, but men in the boat fired a 'Very' pistol which was seen from the destroyer.

All the men on the raft behaved remarkably well indeed throughout this very terrible ordeal and I have nothing but the highest praise for them.

W.P. Boylan

TALE OF THE THREE COUSINS

For the early part of 1942 my father, Robert Carter, along with his two cousins Charley and Tony Workman, were donkey greasers aboard the Canadian Pacific steamer 'Wiinnipeg II'. Most of the rest of the crowd aboard were either from Scotland Road or Bootle. In convoy, six days out of Liverpool for New York they were having a smoke prior to doing 8pm - 12pm watch and actually saw the U-boat in among the convoy. Shortly afterwards they were sunk with no loss of life and all were rescued by a Canadian corvette and landed at Halifax, Nova Scotia, where they were housed in a large wooden mission which also contained other shipwrecked seamen. They were issued with clothes and toilet gear and were very well looked after for six weeks.

When they left, Tony Workman, as he was the youngest and was a fireman, was needed on a Sam boat in Montreal. My father and Charley Workman were sent across Canada by Canadian Pacific Railways (which took them four days) to Vancouver, where the vessel 'Fort Biloxi' was needing two donkey greasers.

They sailed home via the Panama Canal and arrived home about a week earlier than their cousin Tony. So their trip consisted of six days outbound and nearly six months homeward bound! Incidentally, the mission they stayed at in Halifax accidentally burned down with great loss of life, so I suppose they could say they were as lucky as any who survived the war.

Robert Carter Jnr
on behalf of Robert Carter
Anthony Workman & C Workman (deceased)

THE MARITIME ROYAL ARTILLERY

My husband served in the Maritime Royal Artillery and many men were lost serving in that regiment. It is only fairly recently that many people became aware of its existence. The men were mostly men who had been in the Royal Artillery and volunteered when asked, as my husband did, having formerly been in the Royal Horse Artillery stationed at Woolwich, Salisbury Plain etc. The headquarters of the regiment was in the "Bold House", Lord Street, Southport. They were also billeted in several of the large Victorian houses in Alexandra Road and Weld Road, Southport. They slept in Upper Warwick Street, Liverpool when they were due to sail from Liverpool as there were no beds or bunks, they slept on the floor with their greatcoats over them. This place is marked on the old Liverpool maps as 'Drill Hall' and, as I have said, it was at the top of Upper Warwick Street, Liverpool.

The regiment was formed as the merchant ships had to be fitted with guns and they wanted trained gunners to man them. My husband was just one of many who went to Murmansk, Several of the men have recently put in for their medal for this trip and have received it after fifty years, but my husband is not really interested in receiving one.

I don't think the Maritime Regiment had their own cap badge but I can remember sewing a 'flash' on the battledress sleeve, I know it had an anchor on it but I can't remember anything else.

Mrs J Clews

NICHOLAS MONSARRAT AND SEAMAN WALSH

My uncle, John Walsh, was on escort durty in the Atlantic. His ship was a Flower Class corvette - HMS 'Campanula'. His captain was Nicholas Monsarrat, who later wrote "The Cruel Sea". My uncle was the ASDIC Operator, and was in close contact with the captain. In Nicholas Monsarrat's first book ,'Three Corvettes' (1945) my uncle was mentioned.

When going back from leave, my grandmother would always give him a 'salt fish' to take with him. In 'Three Corvettes' the author states that 'Seaman Walsh is complaining that some (-) body has nicked his 'Salt Dolly!'

Sadly my uncle contracted T. B. from the conditions in these small crafts, as did many others.

He died just short of his 30th birthday.

Mrs A Curran

Q SHIP MYSTERY

In the archives of the Liverpool Echo, around November 1942, there are three mentions of a Liverpool mystery 'Q' ship. The first is, 'Mystery Q ship sinks U-boat'; the second is, 'Mystery Q ship scores again' and the third is 'Mystery Q ship vanishes'.

The ship was eventually lured into 'a wolf pack ' of U-boats and took a severe battering. It survived to limp into Lisbon harbour with a skeleton crew. Several of the crew were killed, my father being one of them. One of the deck officers who came from Crosby was decorated for bravery. My mother and I tried to get the full story about the ship through the Admiralty, the Red Cross Society and the Shipping Company but were always told, 'It is a secret of war'. The ship was called 'Lalande', and was at the time registered with Lamport and Holt.

Richard Dutton

MEMORIES OF A BRAVE FATHER

My father, Captain William Nash, MBE, served throughout both World Wars with distinction. After leaving Dublin Nautical School he was apprenticed in sail at the age of sixteen, joining the four masted barque 'Lord Shaftesbury', which belonged to John Herron of Liverpool, in December 1902. I still have his apprentice's indenture, references and medals.

During the First World War, Captain Nash was torpedoed when in convoy from England to Malta but survived to see action throughout the rest of the war. He was torpedoed early on in the Second World War, but, again survived to serve throughout the conflict. His many tours of duty included the dangerous North African run, carrying cargoes of aviation fuel and ammunition. In recognition of his services, he received the North African Star with clasp and was finally awarded the MBE.

After the war he sailed for the British and Continental Steamship Co. Ltd of Liverpool and was a Master Mariner for 32 years of his 50 years at sea. I remember him as a very brave man who, like many others, saw his experiences during those difficult years as part of his normal job.

Mrs W Harland

THE LOSS OF THE 'LACONIA'

The 'Laconia', when approximately 500 miles off Cape Palmas, Liberia (South Atlantic), on a voyage from Suez to the United Kingdom (1,793 Italian prisoners of war, 760 British military and civilian passengers, crew of 692), on September 12, 1942, was attacked and hit by two torpedoes from the German submarine, "U-156" (Korvett-Kapitan, Werner Hartenstein) at 22.07 hrs, finally sinking at 23.25 hrs.

As the stricken liner began to be abandoned, the Germans observed the huge number of people involved and on investigation were horrified to find the large number of Italian prisoners of war (their allies) and civilian personnel aboard.

Kap. Hartenstein informed German High Command of the position of the rescue, He received a reply to assist in rescuing survivors and was told that a number of German and Italian submarines were being sent to assist, and that the Vichy French Government had ordered three naval vessels to be sent from Dakar to take survivors from U-boats (the "U-156" also radioed any ships, allied or neutral to come to the given position). (Promise of safe passage had been guaranteed by German Naval Command to any British or allied vessel that took part in the rescue. Regrettably, no vessels came to the rescue from the allied or neutral side).

A burial at sea from H.M.S. Bermuda - a sight that became part of many sailors' experiences.

"U-156" took many survivors on board, mostly women and younger passengers, The remaining ships' lifeboats were organised into a system of order and upon the arrival of other U-boats, survivors were taken on board at times and given the best possible attention. The people unable to get into the lifeboats, were able to be fed at times and take turns in resting in boards where available. The conduct of the German U-boat crews to the British, Italian and also a large draft of Polish military men was exemplary. The surfaced U-boats displayed large red crosses and from certain lifeboats large sheets with red crosses painted on were laid out, for aircraft to observe.

On 16th September some days after rescue with submarines in attendance on the lifeboats (in fact, towing some) an unidentified aircraft appeared and signals from submarine and from lifeboats to aircraft ensued. The aircraft veered off and suddenly started to strafe the U-boats, in consequence of which some lifeboats were damaged and the occupants injured - some fatally.

The attack continued and, tragically, the survivors on the U-boats had to be put into the sea to facilitate submerging. "U-156" had almost 200 survivors on board at the time of the attack by aircraft. The U-boats submerged and left the area as speedily as possible. The survivors in the lifeboats and the poor unfortunate ones in the water were at the mercy of the sea.

However, the Vichy French had been given the position of the sinking and the three naval ships were on their way, Unfortunately the lifeboats began to disperse and it was a case of individual survival. The loss of life through the attack by aircraft which caused the Germans to leave the rescue scene was appalling; some boats drifted away never to be seen again.

The first French vessel to arrive at the area , was the French cruiser 'Gloire'. She picked up 1,041 survivors, taking them to Dakar. The other two French vessels, sloop, 'Dumont D'Urville' and patrol boat 'Annamite' picked up some more survivors. 40 Italian prisoners of war were taken from the Italian submarine 'Capellini' which at the time of the rescue was on an operational mission against allied shipping in the Atlantic. As it was not practical to keep them on board, they were taken to Dakar as well. One lifeboat, when found, had only four people alive,in once full boat; its occupants had died through thirst, exposure or from injuries received during the ordeal.

Another lifeboat drifted for almost thirty days and reached safety on a stretch of African beach; twenty six men and two women, all suffering from thirst and exposure to sun, had managed to remain alive.

Of those on board the "Laconia" at the time of sinking, approximately 1,000 Italian prisoners of war lost their lives. The deaths amongst passengers, civilian and military were very high. The total number of crew members who lost their lives was 139. (Captain Sharp included).

In regard to the aircraft attack, the German High Command informed the Red Cross in Geneva of the incident. Although the Allies denied the report, the evidence of British and other survivors bore witness to it.

It was not until 1963 that the evidence came to light; in fact the aircraft was,a 'Liberator' from the 343rd Bomber Hay, U.S.A.A.F. based at Ascension Island. The Commander of the Bomber Squadron was Colonel R. Richardson. He was later to become a General of the United States Army attached to N.A.T.O. in Europe after World War II.

The Americans must have realised the terrible events they had witnessed but no attempts were made to investigate the survival area. It is hard to understand the reason for the American denial of knowledge.

The outcome of this attack by the American aircraft was that the German High Command gave orders that in future, no German submarine would assist any vessel that she had sunk, owing to a possible repetition of what happened to "U-156" and other submarines.

Regarding "U-156," commissioned into U-boat Flotilla No; 2 in September, 1941, she was commanded throughout her active career by Korvett-Kapitan Werner Hartenstein.

On leaving the scene of the sinking of the "Laconia", "U-156" encountered the British vessel, "Quebec City" 1927/4,745 tons, owned by Sir W. Reardon Smith, Cardiff, on September 19, 1942. "U-156" sank this vessel, North of Ascension island, by torpedo and gunfire.

This proved to be the last success of "U-156" and Hartenstein returned to Lorient. After repairs he sailed in February of 1943 to the Caribbean to harass allied shipping. However, before meeting any success "U-156" was sunk by a Catalina aircraft of the United States in the Caribbean on 8th march, 1943 (Kor-Kap Hartenstein and his entire crew perished).

In all, from 16 February 1942 until her last success on 19 September, 1942 "U-156" under Hartenstein sank 19 ships of 92,889 tons and damaged 3 at 11,959 tons.

The Italian submarine "Capellini" which saved many prisoners of war, was serving with German U-boats in the Indian Ocean area, based at Singapore in September, 1943 when Italy surrendered. She was taken over by the German Navy and renamed "UIT-24". In May 1945 at the surrender of Germany, she was taken over by the Japanese and renamed "L—", and at the time of the Japanese surrender on August was at Kobe, Japan. In April, 1946 she was scuttled by the allies in a surrender agreement.

(During the period from the first success in October 1940 to the last success in May, 1942, "Capellini" sank 5 ships totalling 31,375 tons. No successes whilst serving as German or Japanese submarine 1943-45).

In memory of James and Edward Hearity of Kirkdale, Liverpool who lost their lives during the sinking of the SS "Laconia", September, 12, 1942.

HMS 'LOOSESTRIPE'

My husband, William John Horn, served aboard the 'Flower Class' corvette HMS 'Loosestripe' as a telegraphist during the Battle of the Atlantic and had vivid memories of an action - known as the 'Night of the Party' which took place on the night of May 5/6, 1943. In fact, he always claimed he was the first to see the U-boat and that he drew his pals' attention to it. They started firing right away. The submarine quickly crash dived and the 'Loosestripe' released depth charges. Everyone was jumping up and down with excitement until someone pointed out two torpedoes which the submarine had managed to fire and which narrowly missed the ship. Up to thirty U-boats were engaged that night, four or five were sunk and another ten or so badly damaged. Many people consider the events of that night to have finally tipped the scales in favour of the Allied convoys and against the U-boats. Four medals were awarded for heroism during the battle and I still have two brass shell cases from the ship and a copy of the telegram sent by Winston Churchill to congratulate the crew of the 'Loosestripe' on their success in sinking an enemy submarine. It just said, 'Splice the Mainbrace!'

My husband had many memories of the Battle of the Atlantic. Once a ship in his convoy was sunk and he saw one man come to the surface clinging to a rope with his teeth!-both his arms had been broken. Fortunately they were strong teeth and he was able to hold on until he was rescued. On another occasion a look -out on my husband's ship spotted a small boat out at sea. The look -out was a New Zealander who was used to fishing off the coast of New Zealand and whose sharp eyes had spotted the tiny dot in the distance. There were only two people in the boat - an 18 year old sailor and his dead captain. They had been adrift for 30 days with a number of others who had died one by one. Sadly, the sole survivor died the next day. My husband was most upset and I still have a photograph of the unfortunate young man's burial at sea.

Back in Liverpool, my husband received a lot of attention; often money would be pressed into his hand - which he would reluctantly accept - and people would touch his collar for luck (an old Liverpool custom). I remember going to the Victory Ball at the Town Hall after the war. There were crowds right down to the Pier Head. We had lost our home in the Blitz and my husband only had his uniform to wear, so, when our taxi driver kept the interior lights on, the people lining the street, seeing a sailor inside, cheered us all the way to the Town Hall.

Ann Horn

TOGETHER

I want to write about my brother Thomas Kavanagh and his three friends, John Barret, Freddie Hill and ... Price (Christian name unknown). These boys were all sixteen years of age when they went to sea. They played together, went to school together, went to sea together and eventually all died together.

They sailed on a ship called the 'Almeda Star' of the Blue Star Line. The ship made three attempts to sail before setting off to the Battle of the Atlantic. The first attempt had been stopped by engine trouble and the second by bombing. The ship did not return.

My grandmother, whom my brother lived with at the time, received a telegram to say that the ship was missing but she did not find out until the end of the war whether they had been taken prisoner or were dead. They did not get any Battle of the Atlantic medals.

Thomas Kavanagh has three sisters and a brother who will never forget him.

J Kavanagh

JUST ONE MORE TRIP

'Ay, lad, don't go.Why don't you miss a trip?' John's wife pleaded with her husband. 'You've done your bit, let the younger lads have a go'. John shrugged his shoulders. 'Just one more trip, Edith,' he said.

John was a veteran of the First World War; an escapee from the cruel communist rule in Russia. He had sailed the seven seas all his life. He was a ships' carpenter and good at his job. He could turn his hand to anything; the sea was in his blood.

His present route was across the Atlantic to Canada. The convoy was taking the ships out of the Mersey straddled miles, and many were the scares as U-boats were detected. On John's ship, children were being evacuated out of England to safer lands to escape the bombings endured nightly by ordinary folk.

John had already been on one journey to Canada with children. He had been struck by the poignancy of the younger children when boat drill was called. They were like sheep standing around, mostly in the dark, shivering, crying bitterly; the very young ones clinging to the older children. They were herded on deck with life jackets, not knowing what was happening.

This last trip went according to plan until they were just off the shore of Newfoundland when the alarm sounded - U-boat detected! Panic ensued, although orderly; the children were terrified, running first to one sailor, then another. This was no ordinary drill. The lifeboats were lowered and the children somehow deposited into the little boats, some crying bitterly for their mothers.

It was a freezing day and a keen wind blew across the treacherous waters. As the little boats drifted away the crew were apprehensive. After about half an hour in the turbulent waters the 'All Clear' came and the task of getting the children back on board and settled down in the warmth commenced.

This was a false alarm, but there were many ships torpedoed on this run.

John did just one more trip from Liverpool to Newfoundland, then retired. Although he had experienced some bad crossings in his time, he could not stand seeing those little children and listening to their pitiful cried.

Mrs Mary J Kivi

CAPTAIN THOMAS ARTHUR MCVEIGH MBE - (MASTER MARINER)

Born in Liverpool, Tom, my eldest brother, left school at the age of fourteen in the middle of the First World War with only one ambition - to go to sea. My father discouraged him because of the danger of being torpedoed by German U-boats at that time. Reluctantly, Tom tried eight different jobs in the space of a few weeks but couldn't stick any of them until eventually he arrive home to say he had been offered a job as a bell boy on the Canadian Pacific Liner SS 'Melita' if he could produce his birth certificate. By this time, dad could see that he had given shore jobs a good try so he gave way and encouraged Tom to go to sea.

Tom sailed next day for New York on the 'Melita' and made several round trips bringing U.S. troops bound for the Western front. On one trip they found a young stowaway on board shortly after the ship left New York. He was made to work his passage across, sharing Tom's duties and his berth, and became quite popular. When Tom came to sign on again at 10.00 o'clock to sail at midnight he was told, ' Sorry son, there's no job for you, we're signing on the stowaway to take him back to new York'.

Tom took his disappointment on the chin, and next day went straight down to the Cunard offices to seek another success! He was taken on as bell boy on the famous SS 'Carmania' which had recently won fame on the high seas for engaging and sinking the German cruiser 'Cap Trafalgar'.

He made sixteen round trips to New York on the 'Carmania' bringing troops to Liverpool, and when the war was over he marched in the Victory Parade through the streets of London.

After the war, Tom gained experience on tugs in the Mersey and sailed as a deck boy on the three masted schooner 'Venus', making several trips to the Hebridies of Scotland via the port of Douglas, I.O.M. and Youghal, Ireland.

By this time he was seventeen and as he had a very good pay book which recorded his deep sea and sailing experience and good conduct, he was taken on by the British and Irish Steam Packet Company as a cadet.

By the time he was twenty four he had all his Mate's and his Master's certificates and was subsequently given command of many Coast Lines' ships including their most up to date vessel, MV 'Innisfallen'.

During the Second World War, Tom had several brushes with German aircraft including a narrow escape when the 'Innisfallen' received a direct hit during an air- raid and was sunk in the Mersey.

It was in February 1942 when Tom was Captain of the MV 'Monmouth Coast' sailing up the Irish Sea to Liverpool, in daylight , that his ship was attacked by two German planes for almost half an hour. Their only defence was two Hotchkiss guns, one each side of the bridge, but they put up a spirited defence with Tom on the bridge in full command directing operations, taking evasive action, changing course sharply and shouting encouragement to his crew and gunners each time the aircraft swooped to bomb and strafe them with machine gun bullets. Sad to relate, one of the gunners was killed but not before both Heinkels were hit by the steady fire of the ships Hotchkiss guns.

The two planes were beaten off and the battered 'Monmouth Coast' limped up the Mersey safely into port to a tremendous rally from the quayside dock workers and the Company's staff who had received news of the action by radio. Parts of the Heinkel aircraft were washed ashore off Dunmore East, Co Waterford, a few days later.

Tom was awarded the MBE for his part in the action, and his surviving gunner received the BEM. I had the pleasure of attending the investiture at Buckingham Palace, with my late wife Marie, to see H M King George VI pin the medal on him.

The citation read:

> "To be an Additional Member of the Civil Division of the Most Excellent Order of the British Empire:
>
> Captain Thomas Arthur McVeigh, Master.

The ship was sailing alone when she was attacked by two German aircraft. Although bombs fell close and badly shook the ship, her Master had organised so sound a defence that the assaults, which lasted altogether nearly half an hour, failed. Petley fired coolly and well. He certainly damaged, and may have destroyed one of the enemy. The ship fought a most determined and successful action and the Master brought her safely to port".

I felt extremely proud of Tom and have always acknowledged him as the hero of our family.

Anthony McVeigh

THE BATTLE OF THE ATLANTIC AND REAR ADMIRAL LEONARD WARREN MURRAY

As Commander-in-Chief Canadian Northwest Atlantic, Rear Admiral Leonard Warren Murray CB CBE, Royal Canadian Navy, was the only Canadian in World War II to hold an independent command in a vital theatre of war in which the enemy was actively engaged.

He was born in Pictou county, Nova Scotia, Canada in 1896 near where his Scots forefathers had landed having sailed from Scotland in the late 1700's. In 1911 he attended the fledgling Royal Naval College of Canada and saw his first action as Midshipman in HMS 'Berwick' during the Mexican Revolution. He passed out in 1914 and over the next few years served aboard HMCS 'Rainbow', HMCS 'Niobe', HMS 'Leviathan' and HMS 'Agincourt'. The by then Lieutenant Murray was present aboard HMS 'Agincourt' at the surrender of the German High Seas Fleet at the end of the Great War.

Between the wars, Admiral Murray qualified in navigation and served in various British and Canadian ships as Navigating Officer, 1st Lieutenant and later as Commanding Officer including HMCS 'Aurora', HMCS 'Stadacona', HMCS Saguenay, HMS 'Queen Elizabeth', HMCS 'Iron

Duke' and HMS 'Tiger'. As befits a career naval officer of that time, he also held various staff posts including Senior Naval Officer, Equimalt, British Colombia, Naval Staff Officer in the Department of National Defence and Senior Naval Officer and Commander in Charge of the Dockyard in Halifax, Nova Scotia. From 1936 to 1938 he served in Admiralty Operations and attended the Imperial Defence College. In 1938 he was appointed Director of Naval Operations and Training at Naval Service Headquarters.

In 1939 he became Deputy Chief of the Naval Staff and during this time attended the Joint Chiefs of Staff meetings leading up to the Ogdensburg Agreement of 1940. He was also one of the first members of the Permanent Joint Board of Defence. In 1940, as a Commodore he commanded HMCS 'Assiniboine' and was named Senior Naval Officer for Halifax Force. In 1941 he held the post of Commodore Commanding Canadian Ships and Establishments in the United Kingdom. On the 13 June, Commodore Murray assumed command of the new escort base as Commodore Commanding Newfoundland Force, the largest naval operational appointment held by a Canadian national to that point in time. By the end of the year, he was promoted to Rear Admiral and became Flag Officer Newfoundland Force. In September of 1942 he became Commanding Officer Atlantic Coast. In April of 1943 as a result of a direct petition from the Prime Minister of Canada, W. L. MacKenzie King to His Majesty King George VI, Rear Admiral Murray was appointed Commander-in-Chief Canadian Northwest Atlantic.

His task as C-in-C was considerable. At the start of the war, Canada had around 1,000 officers, men and reservists in the Royal Canadian Navy and only some six destroyers and a few mine- sweepers. By the end of the war Canada's Navy was one of the World's largest with over 100,000 officers and men and 500 ships in commission including two merchant ships adapted to operate aircraft. Canada also built her own warships for the first time, turning out around 122 corvettes and 60 frigates during the war. The Royal Canadian Navy became highly specialised as it was almost exclusively dedicated to anti-submarine operations and by 1942 Canada was responsible for about 45% of the total North Atlantic escort force. Halifax in Nova Scotia, Canada, has always been of strategic importance as it is the most northerly port on the Western Atlantic seaboard that does not 'ice up' in winter. It was from here that Admiral Murray conducted his campaign from his map - hung office; sometimes working around the clock receiving intelligence reports, personally debriefing his captains and making the crucial decisions necessary to support the supply routes to Europe. The merchantmen he had to escort were always going to be slow moving targets for the U-boats and as the picket lines of U-boats increased he changed the strategy from evasion to attack. With the co-operation of the Royal Canadian Air Force an air umbrella would scatter the U-boat packs and the fast new escort ships would then prosecute any contacts that dared move back towards the convoy.

At the end of the war, Rear Admiral Murray retired to England where he studied law, was called to the Bar and conducted an active practice. Throughout his life he played rugger, soccer and ice hockey, skied until he was 65 and competed in yachting regattas right up to the year before he died. He was active in local politics in Buxton, Derbyshire, where he settled, and of course was a major supporter of the Sea Cadets. He died peacefully at home on 25 November 1971.

Admiral Murray is survived by his widow Dr, Nina Murray, an eye surgeon. From his first marriage to Jean Falconer Scott of St. Catherine's, Ontario, he had two sons (both deceased), William Alexander Scott and Alastair Hugh Garnett. They served in the Royal Navy and William Alexander Scott saw action in the same theatre of war as his father as a young midshipman on convoys to Murmansk, Russia. The younger son later saw action with the Fleet Air Arm at the end of the Korean war, in the Suez crisis and Malaya.

I was 10 years old when my grandfather died. Children often have a clarity of perspective and while I remember him as a very warm hearted and friendly figure his credentials as a 'real seadog' were firmly established when I discovered he was missing the third finger on his left hand- a boating accident in childhood!

Admiral Murray would wish us to remember and pay the highest tributes to the many men under his command who made such sacrifices in their service to the Canadian effort in the Atlantic Campaign. Sacrifices which often meant their own very young lives. Out there the tiny corvettes and their merchantmen charges faced the threat of U-boats, air attack and mines 24 hours a day as they worked back and forth across the North Atlantic. If we add to all this the factor of extreme weather with the risk of capsize from ice build-up on the ships decks we are faced with the fact that this was indeed a very special and brave breed of men.

Rupert Murray,

MY FATHER - CHARLES ERIC ROBINSON

The Anderson shelter put in the garden promptly filled with water and when Dad came home he was horrified that we (Mum, my sister and I)

Rear Admiral Leonard Warren Murray

"Admiral Murray (left) photographed with Admiral Roger Bidwell (then Captain Bidwell) was the only Canadian in World War II to hold an independent command in a vital theatre of war....."

used to get under the dining room table when the air -raid sirens went, so we set about turning the shelter into a 1915 type dugout. Short of a direct hit we were as safe as it was possible to be.

When Dad came home after nine to twelve month trips he brought 1 cwt bags of sugar and white flour, tins of yeast, fruit, fish, meat etc., and we had white home baked bread and black and red currant jam from the fruit bushes in the garden.

After being discharged from the Merchant Navy because of wounds he had suffered when his ship was torpedoed in the Atlantic, Dad came home. It was strange at first having my father home every evening and it was only during this comparatively short time that I got to know him. The Captain's wife and the First Mate's wife visited him; it was a very sad occasion and I can remember him giving both ladies bunches of flowers out of the garden.

When I came home from India the 'Georgic' tied up at Princes Landing Stage. I was at the rails overlooking the stage when I spotted Dad in the company of two Army officers, I caught his attention and he signalled that I was coming ashore.' Ginger 'Reeves who had been at GHQ, New Dehli with me, asked who the Admiral was-Dad was back in Merchant Navy uniform with 3½ rows of ribbons! When I got onto the quay there was much saluting and handshakes but I had to be back on board by 23.59 hours. The only reason I was allowed ashore was because Dad was joining the 'City of Birkenhead' two days later.

In spite of having experienced the 'Cruel Sea' and the harrowing experience of losing all but himself and one other member of the entire ship's crew, Dad, he, like many mariners, could not settle to a 'land lubber's' life and decided to go back to sea. One of the saddest moments of my life was when the Victualling Superintendent called at the house and informed me that Dad had passed away in Sydney Harbour aboard the' City of Birkenhead' and I had to tell Mum and my sister.

C E J Robinson

A NARROW ESCAPE

In March, 1942, at the age of 16, I signed on the 'Kristianfjord', a Norwegian cargo ship sailing from Birkenhead. There were five of us who were local lads whilst the rest of the crew were Norwegian. On that first trip, I sailed to Capetown; from there to Bombay and then back to Capetown. My next trip saw me heading for the West Indies and I arrived at Port of Spain, Trinidad, after 24 days at sea. At the age of 17 I left the

'Kristianfjord' in New York and joined another Norwegian ship, the 'Garnes' as an ordinary seaman for a trip to Nova Scotia and back. I then signed on the Norwegian tanker 'Minister Weddel', again as an ordinary seaman. From New York the 'Minister Weddel' sailed to Port of Spain to take on a cargo of oil. The ship spent Christmas 1942 there and we were able to go ashore and celebrate in true Norwegian style!

After Christmas the 'Minister Weddell' left in a convoy bound for Gibraltar. There were nine tankers in two rows of four and five. Our ship was in the second row on the port side with an escort of one destroyer and three corvettes. One night, shortly after New Year 1943, the alarm went off. I rushed up on deck and saw that a tanker in the front row had been torpedoed and was burning from stem to stern. In the light of the fire I could see a U-boat on the surface. The escort vessels were scurrying about firing star shells and dropping depth charges. The attack continued until dawn and I cannot recall exactly how many tankers were hit on that first night.

It was the second or third attack that accounted for the 'Minister Weddel'. As we were carrying fuel oil, the ship did not go on fire and we were able to take to the lifeboats. Fortunately, there were no casualties at all. At daybreak, the destroyer 'H88' came into view and picked us all up. Attacks continued while we were on 'H88' and I believe that the escort vessels had run out of depth charges! On the last night of the battle another tanker was torpedoed.

On the following day more escort ships arrived to see us into Gibraltar. The crew of the 'H88' kept us informed, telling us that Lord Haw Haw had been giving a running commentary of the battle on the radio, and that they had knocked out up to six U-boats themselves! Once in Gibraltar we transferred to troopship and were kitted out with a few clothes and allowed to send a coded telegram home. We docked at Glasgow and I finally arrived home late at night dressed in a naval boiler suit and overcoat. My dad was working a night shift but my Mum was in. Although she had received my telegram, she did not realise that my ship had been torpedoed and sunk. I had been away for eleven months.

I crossed the North Atlantic many times after that, mainly in British tankers, but I never came under attack again. Once though, my ship was thrown out of a convoy for making too much smoke and on one crossing we were in collision with another tanker.

Jack Sprague

UNCLE TOMMY AND AUNT SUE

As a youngster of 15 years, my uncle Tommy served in the Royal Navy and was at the Battle of Jutland in 1916. After the first World War he joined the Merchant Navy and was still going to sea when war broke out again in 1939.

Early in the war Uncle Tommy's ship was torpedoed and, along with many other seamen, he was taken prisoner and incarcerated on the German ship 'Altmark', anchored in the Norwegian fjords. He was eventually rescued by the Royal Navy and when he returned home all the family pleaded with him to stay ashore but he refused.

When he wasn't at sea, Uncle Tommy lived with his sister, my Aunt Sue, who used to stay with us every weekend when he was away. One Saturday, during the terrible Blitz, she didn't arrive and my younger brother went to her house to see if she was ill. As he got near he could see that there was a huge crater where the house used to be. My brother tried to find out what had happened to Aunt Sue but an air-raid warden would only tell him to fetch his father. When my father arrived, he was told that Aunt Sue was missing and was asked if he would try to identify her from casualties temporarily stored in a number of schools. My father looked at many bodies without success and was eventually shown into a room that had just parts of bodies in it. He was then able to identify Aunt Sue's head - on its own.

Despite the distress caused by this incident, my father's one thought was that Uncle Tommy should not go straight home when he docked. Dad wrote a note telling him to come to our house first and took it down to the shipping office. When the clerk saw the name of the ship on the envelope she called the manager. Uncle Tommy's ship had been sunk. He had been rescued by another ship but, by a terrible twist of fate, that ship was blown up two days later - the very night that Aunt Sue died. There were no survivors.

Diana Swinfield (nee Lang)

LOST AT SEA

During the Second World War, Liverpool was a God-send to the people of this country as it provided a gateway for ships bringing a life-line of much needed supplies across the Atlantic. The dangers were great and Winston Churchill called the U-boat menace the 'Biggest headache of the war'. U-boats would even wait just outside the Liverpool Bar to attack ships.

Many lives from the city were lost, including my father at the age of 37, leaving my mother expecting another baby. I should have sailed with my father on that fateful voyage but the 'Shipping Pool' as it was called in war-time would not give me the necessary form so I cheated almost certain death.

My father had had a strong premonition that he would not see me again and that he was bound for a 'watery grave'. His ship, the SS 'Ceramic', was torpedoed and sunk in 1942 with the loss of all lives except one; the sole survivor being a soldier called Sapper Munday who was taken aboard the U-boat to tell the tale.

I tried many times to get to sea. I tried to get a position on the 'Empress of Asia' which was sunk at Singapore. Finally, I was called to enlist in the Royal Navy and served as a gunner in merchant ships. It seems like only yesterday that my father sacrificed his life. Just one life from so many that were lost at sea but it still haunts me. But the sacrifices of the brave men who saw action in the Battle of the Atlantic were not in vain, for they ultimately achieved a victory for the free world.

Mr Michael P Towey.

SOUTHERN EMPRESS

On April 30th 1942, my husband Bill joined his first ship, it was the 'Southern Empress', a factory whaler converted into an oil tanker - he was just seventeen.

They left Liverpool in a convoy of many ships and their first destination was New York, USA. Having reached there, they then set sail for Houston and Galveston, Texas. Soon after loading the ship with a cargo of crude oil, they then set sail from Texas to rejoin the convoy.

Not long after leaving, the ship developed engine trouble. Black smoke pouring out of the funnel made it too dangerous for them to continue sailing with the convoy, as it would have been a dead give-away to the enemy. They pulled into New Orleans for repairs and once again they were on their way, but again had to pull in, this time to North Carolina. Repairs done, they sailed for New York, USA where, on arrival, they picked up survivors from a ship that had been torpedoed in the Mexican Gulf.

At last they were ready for England and home, so once again they rejoined the convoy.

They were just off the coast of Newfoundland, when the captain received a warning that U-boats were in the area. On 13 October, 1942 at 8pm. the 'Southern Empress' was hit by a torpedo- it took three of them to sink the ship. The men were thrown into the water and those who were lucky were pulled into lifeboats. Bill was one of them.

45 men out of 125 were lost. This number included some of the survivors that had been picked up in New York.

The U-boat surfaced and the German captain spoke to them. He said, 'You are a casualty of war and I cannot help you'. He then said; 'May God go with you'.

The U-boat submerged and the survivors were tossed around in lifeboats for 12 hours until they were finally picked up by a Norwegian corvette.

They spent two days on board and were treated very well. I still have the jacket the Norwegian sailor put on Bill. They were transferred in mid Atlantic to another tanker and no sooner had they been on board when there was a warning of U-boats. One surfaced and the whole of the crew gave themselves up to the Royal Navy. Soon after, the Royal Navy destroyer sank the submarine. They were on their way home at last.

They finally arrived at Greenock, then on to Liverpool, where Bill was welcomed home with disbelief. His family had been informed that the ship had gone down and he was missing.

'No more sea for you', he was told by his parents. Weeks after, Bill was troopcarrying on the 'Queen Mary'. The words the German captain spoke when he said, 'God go with you' makes me thank God that he did, as my Bill is still here to tell the tale.

Mrs M Worthington

Chapter 3

The Battle Ashore...

The stories of those involved
from a Liverpool base

KEEPING THE LINES OPEN

I lived right through the Blitz in Liverpool as a Post Office telephone engineer and I feel it is important to mention the men who kept the telephone service going when the main exchange was broken down.

If it was not for the skill and dedication of these men, then Derby House could not have functioned as it did. Telephone lines were essential to its operations. I performed a few tasks in Derby House basement myself but the main engineers were; Gerry Alster, Noel Felton, Charlie Heather, Rowland Caldwell (all now deceased) and Frank Donnelly (still alive - aged 81)

Peter Cardle

NO SMOKING!!

My father was caretaker of Derby House, and during the Blitz, when bombs had been falling all around he carried on working in that dusty dirty atmosphere.

We lived in our air raid shelter for nearly two years, so we would go down to bed, instead of going upstairs. As dad got into bed one night, mum said, very sleepily, 'Oh Percy, what have I told you about smoking in bed'. My poor dad was covered in dust, he smelt of smoke from fighting the fires that were caused by the bombs. He looked at my mother angrily but then realised that she must have thought he was smoking because of the smell on his clothes and because she was half asleep herself.

Agnes Parry on behalf of her late father Percy Fullerton

WESTERN APPROACHES - LIVER BUILDINGS

I joined the WRNS in 1941. I worked at HMS 'Eaglet', Western Approaches based at the Liver Buildings. I started as a Wren-writer in the pay office on the 5th floor. DEMS was also on the same floor (Merchant Shipping). We were responsible for the pay of all the crew of the Royal Navy Ships and also the pay of the Royal Canadian Navy from Halifax, Nova Scotia. It was very interesting and I met and made a lot of friends.

When the ships went on the Russian Run, and into other war zones, the sailors would go out fresh faced and after some weeks or months would arrive home with beards!! Sadly of course, a lot did not return home at all - this happened in all war zones.

We would exercise on the roof area at the Liver Buildings and thinking on this also brings back memories of marching and of being on parade and 'inspected' by Eleanor Roosvelt. She seemed a very nice lady!

There was, as everyone knows, a lot of bombing in Liverpool and like everybody else, we would pick our way through the rubble of the city at the end of the day.

I advanced to leading Wren in November 1942 and P O Wren in 1943. We mostly served Flower Class frigates, destroyers, subs and others; there were so many names to remember and yet I seemed to remember them all. We worked on ledgers, no computers then!

I have met and kept in contact with some Wrens since that time. When I was released in 1946 I thought about rejoining but got married later that year, and that was that! I have a lot of both happy and sad memories of that time in my life and am glad of an opportunity to share them.

Mrs H Garton

(ex P O Wren Waring)

HARBOUR MASTER'S OFFICE

I started work in the Harbour Master's Office as a clerk on the berthing desk in 1942. Every morning the representatives of the many shipping companies then in Liverpool came to a meeting in the Harbour Master's personal office to obtain berths for the ship that they expected to arrive in the next convoy. My boss on the berthing desk also attended the meeting. Afterwards he would dictate all of the information to the typists. On completion, a copy was handed to me. I had to ring the Dock Master's Office of each dock to inform them which ships were due to dock and where thy were to berth.

My other job was to keep individual records of each ship in the port, date of arrival, to which dock and where berthed. Also, all subsequent moves of each ship (maybe to dry dock or another berth). were recorded and finally, when they departed to join another convoy outwards. The records of each ship were kept for each visit to Liverpool and were often requested by the Harbour master at the morning meetings. Sadly some of the ships did not return.

One lunch time, one of the Assistant Harbour Masters took one of the typists and myself on the overhead railway as he thought we should see all the docks that we only knew on paper. We went from Gladstone Dock to the Dingle and it was an amazing sight; every dock full and dockers loading and unloading the vessels. I have never forgotten it!

A year or so after the war, the young man I had replaced returned and I was moved to another section until I left to get married in 1955.

Jean Hatton (nee Carr)

DERBY HOUSE SIGNALS ROOM

I have read with great interest of the refurbishment of Derby House - and the Battle of the Atlantic. To me as a W.A.A.F. in Signals, it was known as Group HQ and I worked there late 1944 and 1945 as a Corporal Teleprinter Operator. I mention the word Corporal as it was only the Corporals on Watch who were allowed to handle the signals re subs. They came in five figures codes and were transmitted on to the R.A.F. in the Group by means of setting up a broadcast. This was a large

Outside Derby House - office II - staff to the Commander in Chief assemble in June 1945 for an official end of hostilities photo. Photo courtesy of Bernadette Nolan (nee Hart).

telephone switchboard type with a teleprinter connected to it. Each R.A.F. Station had its own call sign and once acknowledgement had been received from each one in the Group, the messages were transmitted to each station at the same time. Literally 'broadcast'.

The R.A.F. were underneath the Ops room (with N.A.A.F.I. window in the corridor which provided us with the odd biscuit etc.) The W.A.A.F. were stationed in Huyton College and were were taken and brought back into Liverpool after each shift - which if I remember rightly was 18 hours on and 18 hours off. Each morning, the Corporal of the watch had to go up stairs to the Naval and Wing Commanders offices, unlock the doors, close the curtains over the Ops. Room - allow the cleaners in and supervise the cleaning, making sure they didn't 'peep' behind the curtains and then when they had finished close it all up again after drawing back the curtains.

The R.A.F. (who were part of the Signals) were men who had been in West Africa and had returned to England.

Gwen E Howell

WRNS were often an official parade - here Queen Elizabeth (now the Queen Mother) visits Derby House from the Rumford Street entrance.

A DOCK MASTER'S MEMORIES

1.

Mersey Docks and Harbour Board, Dock Gateman, later Head Gateman; Piermaster, and finally Dock Master.

At the height of the Battle of the Atlantic, my husband, Wilfred Leach, was a Dock Gateman on Waterloo, Princes Dock where he had been employed since September 1st 1939, after serving seven years as a merchant seaman.

Early in the war, a Company of Manx territorial soldiers were drafted to man gun emplacements at Pier Head and the central docks. they were all young men with not a cook amongst them. One day, a couple of the young fellows came into the dock office and asked if anybody knew how to make barley soup. The gateman on duty knew little more than the 'terriers' so it was suggested that they put half of the hundredweight sack of barley into the dixie along with the addition of water, carrots, onions, celery and seasoning.

Later on, one of the gateman chanced along to see how the soup was coming on; the poor boys were surrounded by all the available dixies full of swollen barley, which they had had to decant from the first dixie as the barley swelled up and threatened to overflow and engulf the floor of the hut which had been allotted to them. We never heard how well the soup was appreciated, but no doubt the seagulls and the pigeons came in for their fair share.

The company were drafted quickly to Europe and my husband subsequently learned that very few of these young Manxmen returned safely to their homes after Dunkerque.

2.

Within days of the Declaration of War, and my husbands commencement of duty with the Dock Board, the passenger ship SS 'Athenia' was torpedoed off the North West coast of Ireland and many lives were lost. This was the first passenger ship casualty of the war.

3. At the peak of the Battle of the Atlantic. the 'City of Benares' left Liverpool Landing Stage with a full passenger list of prisoners of war and children being evacuated to friends and relatives in Canada. Within three days of leaving the port, the ship was torpedoed with large loss of life; amongst them were the two children of a policeman who worked on the dock estate.

4. At one period, a large number of American tanks arrived by convoy at Canada Dock, and were offloaded for dispersal points throughout the

country. They were fuelled and serviced on the quayside by American engineers. As they moved along, one of the tanks demolished a police hut at the boundary wall of the dock estate.

The on-duty policeman demanded particulars from the driver, thus holding up the movement of the following twenty or more tanks. The American officer in charge of the operation, dashed along the roadway in his jeep to discover the reason for the hold up and shouted to the driver in question 'Get back in your tank, we haven't go time for that!' and to the on-duty policeman he said, 'We'll come back after the bloody war and build you a new hut!' We all know the extend of the 'after the war' build up of Liverpool!

5. The storyline themes of 'Dad's Army' were pretty accurate! At the beginning of the war, planes were being transferred from Northern Ireland to Speke Airport, and were flying in low formation up the centre of the river. They had been cleared at Perch Rock Battery, with a pre-arranged signal which was unfortunately misunderstood at Pier Head and led to twin Lewis machine guns stationed on Bibby's warehouse roof, firing shots at the planes. This in turn triggered off other machine guns either side of the river, and bullets were bouncing off the Pier Head. fortunately , however, none of the planes were hit, but it caused a panic on Princes Dock entrance, where the Dock Gatemen were busy in the course of their duty at the height of the tide and were in the direct line of fire from the guns on the warehouse roof.

6. At the close of hostilities, my husband was on duty when the first German submarine was escorted into Canning Dock after surrendering in the Irish Sea, with its crew still on board. A bonus for the navy in this particular surrender was the capture of the first complete snorkel apparatus, which had proved to be such an asset to German submarines.

Wilfred George Leach

JOINING THE FIRE SERVICE

I was the first volunteer in Liverpool in 1941 to join the Fire Service. I wanted to do switchboard work but the head woman wanted me to use my clerical skills (shorthand, typing etc). I did thirteen hours work each day at HG Fire Station, firewatching etc.

My fiance, Ed. Charles Hopkins, a merchant Navy officer, was on the bridge of the 'Pintail' when it was dive-bombed. He was 22 years old. Also his brother Paddy, aged 20 was torpedoed. He was a powerful swimmer but he swallowed so much oil that he died. These two boys came from Ballina, Co. Mayo. It saddens me that their names are not on the memorial stone at the Pier head.

A McCoy (Mrs)

WESTERN APPROACHES HQ - DERBY HOUSE

Between July 1942 and 1945 I was a Wren at Derby House, Liverpool (Western Approaches HQ).

As a member of the Commander-in-Chiefs office (office II Typing Section) I recall that a daily duty was the 'Situations report'; This secret programme which went out to the ships from the Commander-in-Chief Western Approaches, gave the number of the convoy and the names of the ships in the convoy with instructions as to where they were to rendezvous.

I find it difficult to recall accurate information, but positions were given eg; 160°W 90'N or whatever. Commodore Londonderry was, so far as I remember, the principal addressee.

As a shorthand writer, I was called upon to take notes at top secret meetings attended by many senior naval officers, sometimes involving anti-submarine tactics, but I am sorry to say the technicalities went over my head!

About once a week, each Wren from the office had a late duty and on one of mine, I was summoned to the Commander-in-Chiefs flat (Admiral Sir Max Horton) to take dictation. He invited me into an easy chair and I perched on the edge, notebook in hand. He kindly suggested I relax and sit back (I was probably nervous) whereupon I sank back and my knees came up to my chin!

On another occasion on late duty, Captain Lake (he may have been a Staff Officer; Operations) required an urgent directive to be typed and distributed and this was in connection with a Russian convoy where we had lost some thirty odd ships. He was in a dismal and short-tempered mood and said 'I suppose you know we've lost the war'. he ended his report 'It's Doenitz who's done it'.

(I felt so depressed I went to the canteen and bought a packet of cigarettes although until then I had not smoked; it was some 30 years later that I relinquished the habit!)

Dorothy Oldfield
(ex Leading Wren Carroll)

CHAUFFEUR TO SIR PERCY NOBLE

Norman Robertson became the personal chauffeur of Sir Percy Noble in 1941 and this is his story.

Norman was, in 1940, a supplementary reservist and was called up, given a World War I uniform, a rifle and 15 rounds of ammunition and sent to France. Later, because of illness he returned to England and following discharge, applied for the position of chauffeur with the Admiralty. The car he drove was an Austin Princess. Sir Percy Noble was resident at Derby House, he had a suite of rooms on the first floor overlooking Exchange Flags. Each morning when Norman reported for duty, there was a Royal Marine at Sir Percy's door. (Lesser ranking personnel had a sailor at their door).

Sometimes the order would be to drive to Sefton Park. That would mean that the Admiral was going for a walk, which would take about 15 minutes. Then he would return to the office a little more relaxed.

One day, Norman was asked to deliver a letter to the Dowager Countess of Sefton, who lived at Croxteth Hall. On driving through the grounds he noticed an elderly lady in a 'mac' and hat attending to the flower beds. He went to the house and informed the maid that he had a letter for her ladyship. It turned out that the lady in the 'mac' was the Dowager Countess of Sefton. On reading the letter, she told Norman that the answer was 'Yes'. Sir Percy had asked if he may walk in her grounds!

Norman remembers the Admiral as a pleasant, fair and considerate man. On a long journey to Scotland, the two men sat in the car to eat lunch. The driver receiving a bottle of beer and some sandwiches. When he went anywhere that required money, it was Norman's job to get it from Captain Bude (secretary to the Admiral). 'I would give him 5/- to have his hair cut at the Adelphi. I would also give him 5/- for the collection when he went to a service at the Anglican Cathedral'.

On one occasion, his orders were to take Sir Percy to the Adelphi and collect Sir Winston Churchill and take both of them to Gladstone Dock where Captain Walker awaited them. Norman describes what happened next, 'My car was ready and flying the flag (the cross of St George). Sir Percy entered the hotel and came out with Winston Churchill, who stood on the steps and refused to get in the car as he wanted an open topped car so he could wave to the crowds. An open top Wolsey, owned by the police, was quickly obtained. My problem was to get to Gladstone Dock as quickly as possible to tell Captain Walker what had happened as <u>my</u> car was the signal for them to present arms'.

On many occasions, Norman drove the Admiral to Knowsley Hall to have lunch with Lord Derby and amongst other dignitaries he saw were General Montogomery at Derby House, Charles de Gaulle (whom he drove to Huskisson Dock when the 'Malakand' was there). He drove the Duke of Kent to Gladstone Dock, Sir Dudley Pound (Admiral of the Fleet) to Cammel Laird to a launch or a refit, and A V Alexander, 1st Lord of the Admiralty who opened 'Warship Week' at Wrexham.

Norman's final tale concerned 'Sir Max Horton; Sir Max asked me to recommend a golf course and suggested we took a matelot to act as his caddy, which we did. On arrival at Hoylake Golf Course we found that there were professional caddies available so the matelot and I went for a drink'.

Norman Robertson's (aged 83) story
as told to his friend Pat McEvoy.

MY MEMORIES OF DERBY HOUSE

I went into the WRNS at 17 and, although so young, in no way did I fail to recognise the magnitude of the effort by the combined services. It was spectacularly impressive - a great battle being fought and won in Liverpool. I feel, like many others, that I could write a book about my experiences, but since I must be brief, here are my random memories;

Our great C-in-C Sir Max Horton, I'd meet him every day in his 'civvies', off to play golf at Hoylake - he would return to work all night in the Operations Room at Derby House. His great, glass- fronted office looking directly down onto the 'plot' and across to a large map on the opposite wall. A battery of telephones was on his desk in various colours (green was a scrambler). I always experienced a great sense of awe when going into the Operations Room. This gigantic game of chess!

The Admirals flat was on the second floor of Derby House, overlooking Exchange Flags. He had a black marble bathroom - very 'movie star'. George VI and Queen Elizabeth had lunch there as did Marina of Kent who visited as Commander-in-Chief of the WRNS. On all such occasions, we were on parade. One parade I'll never forget was the one for Captain Walkers funeral, WRNS and naval ratings lined the Dock Road, under the 'Dockers Umbrella'.

Visiting the KGS in Gladstone Dock which I found very forbidding.

Days out on a sloop and a minesweeper .... My family friend Captain Case who died in 1991, was at WATU (Western Approaches Training

Unit) in Exchange Buildings as was Philip Mountbatten; all learning to kill U boats.

Finally, I remember everybody going into Derby House over sand-bags, and past Marine sentries; it all was, and is, part of my life.

Betty Sinclair

Staff from the operations room of Derby House.

MRS C STRINGER (1895 - 1985)
FLOTILLA HOUSE

In November 1939, in response to a War Emergency call from Mr Harold Partington (Town Clerk, Bootle Town Hall) Mrs Catherine Stringer offered temporary billeting to a royal naval Officer, (sub Lt. J. MCrae). This soon increased to 6, then to 10 rotating. Thus began what turned out to be a long association with the Royal Navy. On December 22 1940 these original premises were badly damaged in an air raid.

In response to a request by the Royal Navy, the Bootle Borough War Emergency Committee (District Controller Mr Joe Reilly) requisitioned larger and more suitable premises at 35 Pembroke Road, Bootle. The Royal Navy provided the basic facilities to get it started and Percy Noble named it 'Flotilla House'. It was an imposing house set in its own grounds behind Bootle Town hall, half a mile from the Docks. Mr Jo Reilly and Mr Partington approached Mrs Stringer to run it. An important proviso was that it never closed.

Flotilla House provided accommodation, meals and rest for Royal Naval officers, on turn around from convoy escort duties during the Battle of the Atlantic.

Captain F J Walker stayed at Flotilla House on two occasions during this period, as did many others, including officers from the aircraft carrier 'Indomitable'. (Unfortunately, the original visitor's book has been lost.) However, the Captain Walker Association produced a movie film covering their war history in which they featured Flotilla House.

Throughout the duration of the war Mrs Stringer ran Flotilla House, constantly raising its standards and comforts, until it became something like a small hotel for them. Despite heavy bombing, blast damage and numerous incendiary hits, she cheerfully worked on, clearing up and carrying on. During the worst week (May 1st -7th 1941) when Bootle Town Hall had to be abandoned, the Royal Navy provided emergency facilities when the gas and water supplies failed. Her 'Galley', as she proudly called it, never failed to provide the hot meals on time. Mrs Stringer, with great determination and courage, often working 18 hours a day, stayed at her post and kept Flotilla House open 24 hours a day almost single handed. She never went on leave.

It is only on such an occasion as BA93, fifty years after, that the role of this now largely forgotten woman is recalled.

On de-requisition in 1946, with the help of Mr J Reilly, Mrs Stringer bought this house she had come to know and love and lived there until her death aged 90.

Gervaise Stringer (on behalf of Catherine Stringer)

RAF AT DERBY HOUSE

I was among the personnel moved from Mountbatten Plymouth when Derby House became HQ Western approaches.

I was in the RAF our C/O Air Vice Marshall Robb, Derby House was also HQ 15 group RAF Coastal Command. We operated from bases in Northern Ireland and other west coast bases escorting convoys, attacking enemy aircraft and submarines. We based with Army Anti Aircraft Units Barrage Balloon Units, Fighter groups in the defence of Merseyside during the Blitz.

Derby House Operations Room, photograph by Craig Johnstone of Liverpool Libraries. The Operations Room has been lovingly restored to its former glory. Photographed courtesy of Fred O' Brien.

We shared the Ops room with R.N. personnel, I recall the utter disbelief when HMS Hood was sunk by 'Bismark' and the saddened expressions on the faces of the C- in- C Sir Percy Noble and his staff when signals indicated all hands had been lost, some 1200 I believe. There was, I think three survivors, one of, whom was the actor Esmond Knight, blinded by the shelling.

There were joyous and successful moments too, one, the finding by a Catalina of Coastal Command of the 'Bismark' when through bad weather, fog etc, she'd escaped our attention and was making for home port. The Catalina, though attacked, was able to give the 'Bismarks' position when the R.N. was able to avenge the sinking of HMS Hood by destroying her.

Visitors to Derby House were numerous among the many V.I.P.'s whilst I was stationed there, King George VI, Mr. Churchill, Lord Derby, Lord Woolton, John Winant USA Ambassador.

Fred Whitehurst

AND FINALLY................

WEDDING OF THE YEAR

Not all memories of the Battle of the Atlantic were sad ones. My husband, who was at that time my fiance, was in the Merchant Navy sailing in convoy to America.

In February 1941 we decided to get married (on his next leave) in June of that year. He ordered his wedding suite and I had the task of choosing my wedding dress and also those of my bridesmaids. The family gave their clothes coupon and also their food coupons for the cake and other items needed for the reception. As all the sugar went into the cake, we had to make do with chocolate for the covering.

We went to see the Vicar of St. John's, Knotty Ash, who was very understanding and told us he would marry us as soon as the ship docked, that is, as long as the banns had been read for three Sundays.

My fiance sailed away and everything went well until May 1st, when we had the Liverpool Blitz. It lasted until the 9th and the German bombs rained down, destroying Blacklers. Lewis's was also hit and Saint Luke's Church at the top of Bold Street was burned out by incendiary bombs. The Dingle Jetty and many places along the docks were hit. Meanwhile our wedding plans went ahead.

The bridegrooms suit was delivered to his mothers house in Aigburth, near the Dingle Jetty, and the bride's and bridesmaids dresses were ready in my wardrobe. The cake was ready and only had to have the icing put on. The banns had been read.

News of the Liverpool Blitz was flashed across the Atlantic and the Liverpool men on board the ships were allowed to send a telegram to their relatives asking if they were alright. I received a telegram which read;

"Go along to Ma's and check my suit is OK"

I married him anyway!

J B Lowe